What Practitioners Are Saying About *Teaching Matters Most*

In this new era of "accountability," teachers and administrators are beleaguered by metrics that channel their time and resources into factors that are not only peripheral to the primary mission of a school, but can actually get in the way of meeting this mission. In Teaching Matters Most, *McCann, Jones, and Aronoff remind us that to provide students with the highest quality of education, we must refocus on defining quality in classroom instruction and building support systems for the teachers providing that instruction.*

—Matthew Haug
Principal, Central High School
Burlington, Illinois

I am grateful to the authors of Teaching Matters Most *for their efforts to improve student learning through the examination of classroom instruction. McCann, Jones, and Aronoff offer useful strategies that allow teachers to review their practices through frequent reflection. I especially appreciate the succinct summaries and questions for reflection at the end of each chapter. The book guides staff through activities that focus on their instructional practices in the interest of maximum student learning. Studying this book can be a continuous professional development activity for teachers and school leadership teams.*

—James Pluskota
Principal, Edison School
Elmhurst, Illinois

To the many dedicated teachers who have influenced our lives in countless positive ways and have ultimately positioned us to offer this modest contribution to the community of educators who continue to do important work.

teaching
matters
most

A School Leader's Guide to
IMPROVING CLASSROOM INSTRUCTION

Thomas M. McCann
Alan C. Jones
Gail A. Aronoff
Foreword by Deborah Meier

A Joint Publication

CORWIN
A SAGE Company

learningforward

CORWIN
A SAGE Company

FOR INFORMATION

Corwin
A SAGE Company
2455 Teller Road
Thousand Oaks, California 91320
(800) 233-9936
www.corwin.com

SAGE Publications Ltd.
1 Oliver's Yard
55 City Road
London, EC1Y 1SP
United Kingdom

SAGE Publications India Pvt. Ltd.
B 1/I 1 Mohan Cooperative Industrial Area
Mathura Road, New Delhi
India 110 044

SAGE Publications Asia-Pacific Pte. Ltd.
3 Church Street
#10-04 Samsung Hub
Singapore 049483

Acquisitions Editor: Debra Stollenwerk
Associate Editor: Desirée A. Bartlett
Editorial Assistant: Kimberly Greenberg
Permissions Editor: Adele Hutchinson
Project Editor: Veronica Stapleton
Copy Editor: Diane DiMura
Typesetter: Hurix Systems Pvt. Ltd
Proofreader: Dennis W. Webb
Indexer: Kathleen Paparchontis
Cover Designer: Michael Dubowe

Printed in the United States of America.

Library of Congress Cataloging-in-Publication Data

McCann, Thomas M.

Teaching matters most : a school leader's guide to improving classroom instruction / Thomas M. McCann, Alan C. Jones, Gail A. Aronoff; foreword by Deborah Meier.

A joint publication with Learning Forward.

p. cm.
Includes bibliographical references and index.

ISBN 978-1-4522-0510-6 (pbk.)

1. Teachers—In-service training. 2. School improvement programs. I. Jones, Alan C. II. Aronoff, Gail A. III. Title.

LB1731.M42 2012
370.71'1—dc23

2011052961

This book is printed on acid-free paper.

12 13 14 15 16 10 9 8 7 6 5 4 3 2 1

Contents

Foreword

Yes—as the title says—teaching matters. But, we also know how easy it is for this to become rhetorical rather than reality-based. We are learning all the time—even if the teachers are not always clearly visible. Our teachers come in many forms—including some that we probably view as undesirable. Even the way we organize schools "teaches" us something—requiring silence is a message, no excuses sends a message, but so does chaos. The arrangement of chairs and desks, what's on the walls of a classroom are teaching—whether intentional or not.

It's hard to remember this—maybe especially for teachers who have to spend so much of their time facing (often literally) groups of twenty to forty for forty-five minutes to five hours a day. It sometimes even seems to us that standing back for a few minutes and observing our students is lazy, wasting time, not doing our job. We try to plan while also knowing that the most powerful teaching arises out of connections kids make or don't make to our plans. As no two children are alike, nor no two teachers, the best of all plans often go astray unless we know how to observe closely, be flexible, and respond mindfully.

It's an impossible task, but to my surprise it can be transformative over time, especially so if the school as a whole reinforces the habits of mind and heart that are part of the best classroom. And that the classroom is thought of more broadly—as a school as a whole and the larger society within which it sits. Since we want students to keep learning when they are out of our sight, we need always also to be looking for ways to hook our teaching to their lives.

But students, like teachers, spend a lot of their psychic energy hiding from judgment. That's a fact of life in any hierarchal system where power rests overwhelmingly on one side. Yet feedback is essential. Ways of "seeing" ourselves as teachers through the eyes of others—whether it be video or commentary—is always startling. It can create higher walls or increased openness.

Looking at the work in this book reminds me though that what the authors are describing is time consuming. It's hard enough to find time to plan ahead at all, with awareness that x, y, and z need quick attention before the learners turn off. And then even if the lessons went perfectly, who knows what will remain in the students' repertoire by tomorrow? How can the homework prepare for tomorrow and reinforce today? And when will I read it all? And when will I comment on it in general and to each of my 30–150 students.

But as McCann, Jones, and Aronoff make clear, this is a mere surface measure of time. In fact, we need time to see each other at work, to read about the work of others, to study the research in our discipline as well as our teaching field, to respond to critiques from outside, to look over past records and documents to see how students are progressing and how their work in my room fits into their work elsewhere . . . and when will I find time to talk with x (former teacher, colleague, student . . . and maybe a family or two)?

My daughter told me when she went from being a part-time teacher for seven years to being a fulltime teacher that "it's not possible," she moaned. The standard she had set for herself required at least an hour of preparation, review, and more for every instructional hour.

I kept wishing I could be back in school while a group of teachers digs into some of this stuff and reads out together some of the examples offered of real teachers in action. That's where the task of improving teaching begins, and where we actually learn a lot about what a good teaching/learning environment is, not only for teachers, but also for students. I appreciate the authors' recognition of this connection between our task and theirs.

This book is important in laying out any number of ways for our thinking about what counts most during the time we spend with our students, and it raises simultaneously the questions of how we might reorganize schooling to make these important models doable and effective. To start with, it means providing teachers themselves with a front row in discussions and plans for school organization—better yet—for seats on the stage as designers as well.

—*Deborah Meier*

Preface

Lessons Learned From Experience

Everyone seems to agree—from popular media commentators to government policy makers and academic researchers, including Darling-Hammond and Bransford (2005) and Darling-Hammond and Haselkorn (2009)—that the quality of teaching in classrooms is the single most important factor in advancing student achievement and in sustaining school improvement. Everyone seems to agree that we have to have consistently high-quality teachers in schools. At the same time, we see a jumbled competition of approaches to ensuring that all classrooms have high-quality teachers. Backing each approach is a distinct vision of the function and operation of schools and a distinct understanding of the organization of schools and the psychology of teachers and learners. In *Teaching Matters Most: A School Leader's Guide to Improving Classroom Instruction*, we make the case that the quality of teachers that we place and sustain in classrooms is the single most important factor in continuous school improvement and in any attempt to reform schools. Furthermore, we suggest a path for advancing this goal. This path is not a simple mechanism, but involves a complex of responsibilities and proficiencies from the leadership in schools.

A "NEW" TAKE IN SCHOOL IMPROVEMENT

The actions that we describe in this book might seem to some readers to be fundamental and common to almost all schools. However, we advocate an apparently uncommon practice: that school leaders need to embrace the idea that *teaching matters most* and must act on this principle by leading the school community in a concerted effort that requires the tight alignment among fundamental actions. This includes recruiting, hiring, inducting, mentoring, supporting and delivering meaningful professional development, and evaluating teachers in a manner that recognizes their need for a sense of efficacy, autonomy, and community.

We recognize that procedures and programs for induction, mentoring, professional development, and teacher evaluation should be common to schools, although the quality of the programs might be uneven and unaligned. This book can help school leaders to define the common commitment that could bind these separate elements together, and our advice for action steps could help school leaders to improve any one of the individual components.

Part of our concern is that too often the leaders in schools, while acknowledging the importance of teachers, look to streamlined mechanisms and sometimes to peripheral activities instead of addressing the admittedly messy work of improving the quality of teaching in a school. In this book, we offer an alternative to popular options. Simply put, the alternative requires three key elements:

1. Envisioning what good teaching looks like and sounds like

2. Measuring the quality of current instruction against this standard

3. Working relentlessly in concert with a community of professionals to move the quality of instruction closer and closer to the ideal

Of course, each one of these elements embeds layers of complexity and assumes substantial knowledge and skills on the part of the leaders in any school. And we understand that a myriad of distractions move school leaders away from primary attention to the quality of teaching. Throughout the book, and especially in the last two chapters, we suggest ways to remain focused and to develop the leadership proficiencies necessary to be a strong and steady instructional leader.

When we examined the school improvement plans from a set of randomly selected schools (McCann, Jones, & Aronoff, 2010), we were curious to see the trends among the targets that schools had set for improvement. By and large, the plans in this set focused most attention on propping up areas of deficiency and too often the expressed goals seemed only peripherally connected to the work that teachers do in classrooms. We trust that a committee or an individual administrator conscientiously wrote the school improvement goals, judging that they were significant statements within the particular school contexts. However, we have to ask in each instance, if the goal is aggressively pursued, will it substantively improve the quality of teaching and thereby significantly advance the learning for all students? Too often, our answer is *no.*

CENTRAL THEME

We have worked in public schools for more than a combined one hundred years. We continue to observe in schools as researchers, university supervisors, and consultants. Our thousands of hours of classroom observations have convinced us that schools will not make significant progress in advancing the learning and achievement of all students unless they make significant strides in improving the quality of instruction in all classrooms. With *Teaching Matters Most: A School Leader's Guide to Improving Classroom Instruction*, we argue for renewed and sustained attention to improving the quality of instruction in schools. Furthermore, we insist that schools work against this effort when school leaders focus too much attention on the peripheral matters of schooling that often distract from the core effort to advance learning and improve the quality of students' experiences in classrooms. We understand that students are going to be intellectually engaged and learn at high levels of achievement when they experience consistently high-quality instruction. We propose an approach to school improvement that does not single out struggling subgroups as the focus for correctives. Instead, we offer that schools leaders need to conceive firmly and in substantial detail what good teaching looks like, sounds like, and feels like. They must take the measure of the quality of instruction against this yardstick, and they must work relentlessly to move the quality of instruction closer and closer to the ideal in every classroom.

ORGANIZATION OF THE BOOK

The book begins by making the case for the importance of teaching and for improving the quality of teaching. The chapters that follow report current trends in instruction in schools. The report shows that while teachers are working hard, instruction is often uninspired and rarely challenging or intellectually engaging. We note the current debate about whether or not there are "best practices" in teaching, and make the case that we can say with confidence that some practices are clearly better than others. While we acknowledge that other authorities, for example Danielson (2007) and Stronge (2007), have described quality teaching according to elaborate rubrics, these descriptions make it difficult to sort out the pedagogical priorities. One chapter offers a description of distinctive practices that separate exceptional teachers from mediocre teachers.

Subsequent chapters detail the actions that are necessary to promote and sustain consistently high-quality teaching, including the communication steps needed to initiate the plan. The actions include attention to hiring, recruiting, and induction practices. We suggest the elements that should be part of any mentoring program. We envision what a meaningful staff development program would look like. We propose the necessary steps in a teacher evaluation process that promotes professional growth. We share how attention to what students tell us can inform us about the quality of instruction and the experience in every classroom.

We acknowledge the realistic challenges in following the course that we propose. However, we note that the recognition of challenges does not invite despair. As school administrators, we have taken the stance that recognized challenges are specific problems to be solved, not insurmountable roadblocks. We do not deny that what we propose will be difficult at times and will be quite different from more popular and easily marketable approaches to reform and improvement. At the same time, experience tells us that principals in most schools have a great deal of autonomy to be creative and to translate various mandates into actions that are appropriate for the specific instructional context of their schools. For example, if principals must evaluate and rate all teachers, there are ways of doing this that support the teachers' development and foster reflection.

WHAT MAKES THIS BOOK DISTINCTIVE

It should come as no surprise to you that *teaching matters most* in the sense that the quality of the teaching in a school is the key factor that advances learning, achievement, and student satisfaction. Of course school administrators, board members, and policy makers act on this fact in various and sometimes contradictory ways. Here is what is distinctive about our approach:

- We recognize that school leaders have no control over the *input,* the teacher training that prepares candidates to deliver high-quality instruction and to function well as a member of an instructional team. We see the task before leaders as working with the current reality of the staff and the community where they are situated.
- We see hope in an intense focus on continually working toward the improvement in the quality of teaching across all grades and across all disciplines.
- We insist that the criteria for defining quality teaching cannot be captured in static checklists but must be authored repeatedly

through a collaborative and recursive process with the instructional staff of a school.

- We propose a plan for the alignment of key elements that promote continual improvement of the quality of teaching, all connected by the communitywide understanding of what quality teaching should look like, sound like, and feel like.

- With this book we offer the recommendations and provide the tools that will help school leaders to improve the quality of instruction in schools, leading to more learning, higher achievement, and increased satisfaction for learners and for teachers. We recommend steps for individual components of the instructional program in individual chapters and link the steps into one comprehensive plan represented by a recurring graphic at the end of each chapter.

We see great hope for school improvement through an intense effort to improve the quality of teaching across grades and across subjects. We offer a vision of key characteristics that would distinguish teaching that is engaging, compassionate, coherent, and rigorous. We suggest how to take the measure of the current status of teaching within a school and to check for growth in the quality of teaching over time. The tools that appear in the resources section of the book should help in this effort. We set out a blueprint for how to advance the quality of teaching through an aligned plan that attends to teaching standards and professional growth needs, from recruitment to induction and mentoring to evaluation to ongoing professional development. The hope for significant school improvement and meaningful reform lies with the teachers. The hope for leaders is that they can follow a focused and aligned effort to improve the quality of teaching to impact all learners.

Acknowledgments

A book that celebrates the important impact that teachers have on the lives of learners has to begin with our expression of gratitude to the teachers who have taught us how to be teachers and how to reflect on the qualities that distinguish great teaching. We are most grateful to George Hillocks Jr., John V. Knapp, and Maury Gladstone.

Several mentors over our careers have influenced our thinking about instructional leadership for this book, including George Bieber, Henry Landi, and Richard Kamm. This book benefited from the insightful readings and guidance of distinguished school administrators, including John Carter, James Pluskota, Judy Minor, Lisa Smith, Joyce Powell, and Diana Smith. These leaders reminded us of the reality of schools, the important work of schools, and the crushing demands made on principals and other school administrators. Several school leaders have helped us to appreciate the realistic challenges facing administrators who want to take seriously the improvement of instruction. Among these leaders are Marjorie Appel, Steve Arnold, Maura Bridges, John Carter, Joe Crickard, John Highland, Paul Junkroski, Marianne Melvin, George Strecker, and Lee Yunker.

We also appreciate the recommendations from several anonymous reviewers who are themselves school administrators. Their observations, questions, corrections, and advice helped to shape the book into a more reader-friendly document. We have also relied on the insights and consistent good counsel of Linda Jones, who helped us to explore our ideas and our written product critically.

In thinking about what distinguishes high-quality teaching and why it matters most, we have looked to the examples of exemplary teachers Joseph Flanagan, Larry R. Johannessen, Elizabeth Kahn, Katherine E. McCann, Pam McCann, and Peter Smagorinsky. Our observations of their work and our rich conversations with them about key attributes of distinguished teaching helped us to define for ourselves what characteristics and practices are important. We are also indebted to our teacher certification colleagues Laura Bird, Susan Callahan, Marilee Halpin, Christine Henderson, John Knapp, Jeff Levin, Beth McFarland-Wilson, Brad Peters, and Judy Pokorny. These teachers of teachers embrace the principle that *teaching matters most* and commit themselves to preparing exemplary teachers for the future.

The editors and production staff of Corwin have moved a project idea into a book that we are very proud of. We especially appreciate Deb Stollenwerk for her support for the project from the initial proposal to the completed book. We have relied on her guidance and encouragement throughout the process. We are also grateful to Desiree Bartlett and Kim Greenberg for their gentle prodding and reliable guidance to move the book through the production phase.

PUBLISHER'S ACKNOWLEDGMENTS

Corwin would like to thank the following individuals for taking the time to provide their editorial insight and guidance:

Randel Beaver, Superintendent
Archer City ISD
Archer City, TX

Karen Canfield, Principal
Pioneer Intermediate School
Noble, OK

Sammie Cervantez, Principal
Munsey Elementary School
Bakersfield, CA

Laurie Emery, Principal
Old Vail Middle School
Vail, AZ

Patricia Long Tucker, Superintendent
Altadena, CA

Kathy Tritz-Rhodes, Principal
Marcus-Meriden-Cleghorn Schools
Marcus, IA

Gayle Wahlin, Director of Leadership Services
DuPage Regional Office of Education
Downers Grove, IL

About the Authors

 **Dr. Thomas M. McCann** is an associate professor of English at Northern Illinois University, where he contributes to the teacher certification program. He taught high school for twenty-five years, including seven years working in an alternative high school. He has been a high school English department chair, an assistant principal, and an assistant superintendent. His published work has appeared in *Educational Leadership, Research in the Teaching of English,* the *English Journal,* and the *Illinois English Bulletin.* His coauthored books include *Explorations: Introductory Activities for Literature and Composition, 7–12* (National Council of Teachers of English (NCTE), 1987), *In Case You Teach English: An Interactive Casebook for Preservice and Prospective Teachers* (Merrill/ Prentice Hall, 2002), *Supporting Beginning English Teachers* (NCTE, 2005), and *Talking in Class* (NCTE, 2006). He edited and contributed a chapter to *Reflective Teaching, Reflective Learning* (Heinemann, 2005). He is the coauthor of *The Dynamics of Writing Instruction* (Heinemann, 2010). The NCTE awarded him the Richard A. Meade Award for research about the concerns of beginning teachers. He also received the Paul and Kate Farmer Award from NCTE for his writing for the *English Journal.*

 **Dr. Alan C. Jones** is an Associate Professor of Educational Administration for Saint Xavier University, Chicago, Illinois. His teaching career includes teaching English at DuSable Upper Grade Center in Chicago, Illinois, and social studies at Thornton Township High School in Harvey, Illinois. He began his administrative career as an activities director at Thornton Township High School and went on to become an assistant principal at Bremen Township High School in Illinois and served as principal of Community High School District 94 in West Chicago,

Illinois, for seventeen years. Under his leadership, Community High School was awarded the Blue Ribbon School of Excellence in 1993 and was recognized as a 1995 School of Excellence by *HISPANIC* magazine. His publications include articles in educational journals on instructional leadership and school reform and two books: *Students! Do Not Push Your Teacher Down the Stairs on Friday: A Teacher's Notebook* (Quadrangle Books, 1972) and *Becoming A Strong Instructional Leader: Breaking the Cycle of Reform Failure* (Teachers College Press, 2012).

Ms. Gail A. Aronoff is an educational consultant who worked for thirty-seven years in several schools, both as teacher and administrator. She has worked with students with special needs in elementary, middle school, and high school and served as a liaison between schools and the families of struggling learners. At the high school level, she taught struggling learners for fourteen years and held the position of Assistant Principal for Student Services for twelve years. She served a highly diverse population with many English language learners (ESL students) as well as those from low-income families. She has mentored and supervised teachers and administrators, creating and implementing model programs to address the needs of reluctant learners and those with special needs. Ms. Aronoff currently serves as a consultant to schools for school improvement and reform.

What are common practices in schools? 1

I f we could enter the minds of a superintendent, a principal, and other school leaders as they prepare for the opening of a new school year, we might find them preoccupied with a dizzying array of responsibilities and uncertainties. We know because we have been there ourselves. For example, the superintendent might worry about her personal image, her relationship with members of the school board, her role as motivator to the staff, her political need to advance student achievement and to look competitive when compared to neighboring school districts, the logistics of executing the day's agenda, and much more. A principal or dean might focus on keeping the school safe and orderly, with buses arriving on schedule and students being fed wholesome meals in the cafeteria. A department chair might focus on the competition for technology resources or the current status of a book order. In danger of being lost or subordinated in the web of preparation is overt attention to the core mission of schools: that students will learn, that they will develop their talents, and that they will hone their sense of good character and responsible citizenship. We hardly think that the few school leaders named above are alone in their preoccupations.

When we examined the school improvement plans from twenty randomly selected school districts, we were curious to see the trends among the targets that schools have set for improvement. From our examination, we drew three conclusions: (1) Schools first target the areas identified for measuring adequate yearly progress. Reading is the first concern, with mathematics following as a close second. (2) When schools have not made adequate yearly progress, they target improvement in reading or mathematics for a particular subgroup, especially ethnic or language minorities. (3) In addition to setting sights on increasing achievement in reading and mathematics, schools set goals related to a wide array of concerns and topics, some that one can recognize as related to the core

1

mission of schools, and some that seem more distant. While it is reasonable to aspire to increase student achievement in reading and mathematics, we question the means that schools take to realize this goal, and we especially wonder about the second and third trends listed above.

Consider the seemingly reasonable tendency for schools to try to fix up the underperforming subgroups in an effort to make adequate yearly progress. In our sample, we see statements that express the intention to improve reading and mathematics achievement among African Americans, Latinos, and students from low-income homes. The presumption implied by such goals is that all African Americans, Latinos, and students from low-income homes perform similarly and that everyone else is more or less doing fine. In short, the model calls for correcting the deficient and for letting everyone else carry on. Of course, we question the assumptions, and we haven't seen schools make radical improvements by implementing tactics or interventions to remedy the deficient subgroups. We say more about this difficulty below.

The third trend reveals a kind of fragmented response to significant issues about learning and achievement. Here are some representative goal statements from our sample:

> "Improve the participation of our Hispanic students in the PSAE [Prairie State Achievement Exam] math test."

> "Boost enthusiasm for learning."

> "Engage in courageous conversations."

> "Implement a restructuring plan."

> "Increase enrollment in rigorous programs."

> "Increase stakeholder involvement."

> "Increase professional collaboration."

> "Expand grading by objectives."

> "Implement and maintain consistent school wide initiatives that will adequately increase the graduation rate."

> "Review curriculum in all areas for alignment with College Readiness Skills."

We understand that a committee or an individual administrator conscientiously wrote these goals because they seemed to be significant statements within the particular school contexts. However, we have to ask in each instance if the goal, aggressively pursued, will substantively improve the quality of teaching and thereby significantly advance the learning for all students.

Our work in schools for more than a combined one hundred years, our thousands of hours of observations of classroom instruction as supervisors in schools, and our more recent observations in schools as university supervisors and consultants have convinced us that schools will not make significant progress in advancing the learning and achievement of all students unless they make significant strides in improving the quality of instruction in all classrooms. We urge renewed and sustained attention to improving the quality of instruction in schools. Furthermore, we insist that schools work against this effort when school improvement plans offer a labyrinthine network of initiatives, like having "courageous conversations" and increasing "stakeholder involvement," that touch on the peripheral matters of schooling and often distract from the core effort to advance learning and improve the quality of students' experiences in schools. We understand that students are likely to develop a deep understanding of essential concepts, to learn generative procedures, and to refine complex communications only when they experience quality instruction. We propose an approach to school improvement that does not single out struggling subgroups as the focus for correctives. Instead, we offer that schools need to conceive firmly and in substantial detail what good teaching looks like and sounds like. Schools must take the measure of the quality of instruction against this yardstick, and must work relentlessly to move the quality of instruction closer and closer to the ideal.

WHAT WE FOUND IN CLASSROOMS

In the variety of schools we have visited over a three-year period as outside consultants, we have seen many hard-working teachers who apparently devote much time to planning lessons and who generally enjoy a positive rapport with students. In the classrooms, we have seen cooperative students, apparently willing to learn, and noticeably compliant with the directions of their teachers. We have seen schools rich in diversity, with students representing a variety of social, economic, cultural, and linguistic backgrounds, functioning collaboratively and expressing pride in the harmonious mixture of students in their school. These two factors—conscientious teachers and willing learners—appear to be the basic elements for a formula for a high-achieving student body and a dynamic learning environment.

At the same time, we have witnessed learners enduring compliantly a lot of uninspired instruction, with implied simplistic learning goals, discourse dominated by teacher talk and student recitation, and assessments that placed greatest value on recall of disseminated information. We watched lessons that began *in medias res,* with no foregrounding through a review of previous activities and learning, no preview of subsequent activities and projects, and no explicit expression of current and long-term goals. The students we interviewed expressed some distress that while teachers set tasks and were available at various times to help students complete the tasks, the teachers did not make it easy to navigate the curriculum—the knowing *why* they were engaged in the assignment or project and *where* the work was leading. Indeed, we saw little evidence from classroom observations, from interviews with teachers, or from forums with students, that teachers could convey to students the unifying elements of the curriculum or had a sense themselves of the curriculum as a unified whole. We have to admit that our sample size is small, and the schools we visited across states and across socioeconomic boundaries may not be representative of a mass of schools where high-quality teaching and a commitment to its continual improvement are the norm. But, based on our experience, we judge that any school has a lot of room for improvement in the quality of instruction.

As part of our consultations in schools, we talked to administrators who spoke of magical qualities in the instructional practices in schools, but we failed to see this magic during our hundreds of classroom observations. Teachers testified of the need to have in place a supportive teacher evaluation system that set clear standards for performance and promoted teachers' development toward these benchmarks. We recognized an absence or inconsistent sense of what quality teaching is, making it difficult to know what to look for in hiring, mentoring, supporting, and retaining staff.

In short, what we have witnessed is an enormous potential for rapid improvement in learning in schools, with the concomitant closing of achievement gaps among subgroups of the student population. Most teachers are hard working and knowledgeable about their subjects, and most learners are willing to learn. And the administrators we have met are conscientious, hard working, and even courageous. While critics might be eager to fault everyone in schools for failing to see and do what needs to be done to improve schools dramatically, we find it difficult to fault anyone for failing to see truths hidden in plain view, especially since a variety of external factors conspire to obscure the obvious.

TRUTHS HIDDEN IN PLAIN VIEW

Many schools and the administrators who manage them are under fire. In response to mandates to raise test scores or face dire consequences, school districts rush to implement the programs or "scientifically proven" interventions to advance achievement rapidly in their schools. We say more about this problem in Chapter 2. What is largely ignored in school improvement plans is what goes on in classrooms between teachers and students around subject matter—the truth before our eyes. The reality is that administrators busy themselves with a wide array of responsibilities, and teachers invest precious time in workshops that promise to advance the way they teach. At the same time, the century old assign-and-assess method of instruction remains intact: teachers talk a lot, students listen a lot, and teachers grade a lot. If what we are trying to do in schools is fundamentally change how students write, compute, and think, then the pervasive assign-and-assess method of instruction must not only change but be transformed into a model of teaching. This model must promote quality interactions between teachers, students, and peers. Subject matter must be organized to draw students into disciplined approaches to solving contemporary problems and dilemmas, and assignments must be designed to replicate authentic responses to real-world tasks.

We think we have discovered some fundamental truths that have been hidden in plain sight. First, schools are never going to make substantial gains in improving students' learning and achievement until they emphasize improvement in the quality of teaching across the curriculum. Citing recent research about the relative effects of teacher quality, Darling-Hammond and Haselkorn (2009) affirm that quality instruction from well-prepared teachers has a greater impact on student achievement than "the effects of race and parent education combined" (p. 30).

While schools strive to accelerate learning in the core areas of reading and mathematics for those students who struggle in these areas, the broader challenge is to improve the quality of instruction across a school or across an entire system. The research is clear that the quick fix might lead to transitory gains, but the overall improvement in instructional practices allows schools to boost learning substantially and sustain improvement in an environment of high expectations and high performance.

The second truth we have discovered hidden in plain sight is that students will only learn at high levels when teachers teach. Hillocks (2009b) has called for a "revolution" in literacy instruction (p. 8). To make his case, he cites his study of the impact of various coded activities in hundreds of observed lessons. Trained research assistants designated separate "episodes" within lessons and coded the episodes according to the current activity. Not surprisingly, the more episodes that were coded as diversions (for example, announcements on the public address system, students engaged in social conversation, teacher conferring with a colleague in the hall), the less learning occurred. There was a negative correlation: more diversions, less learning. Perhaps less obvious was that the more teachers devoted time to instruction, especially instruction to advance *procedural knowledge*, the more students learned. This is a positive correlation: the more teaching, the more learning. Time taken up with assessment had less positive impact on learning.

While we are reporting the obvious, we will add a third truth hidden in plain sight. Quality instruction must feature some basic routines, including the rudimentary practices of situating learning in the essential concepts of the curriculum, reminding students about what they have experienced so far, what the current and long-term goals are, and how the current activities will prepare them for subsequent learning and performance. As we have noted earlier, the dominant assign-and-assess model just doesn't work well. As Willingham (2009) suggests, students will engage if they see instruction as a purposeful effort at problem solving, with classroom discourse patterns elevated above mere recitation.

TRANSFORMING ACCOUNTABILITY

Jumping off the treadmill of a decade worth of accountability mandates and attending to the classroom truths children experience each day requires a fundamental change in how we talk about accountability and how we act upon this new conversation. Based on our extensive observations in real classrooms in a variety of schools, we recommend a four-part strategy for transforming the truths in American classrooms.

First, educators must stop using business terminology such as *accountability*, *quality dashboards*, or *metrics* to describe what they do in schools. Unlike typical circumstances in the business sector, the certainties of inputs, outputs, and means of production are not a part nor will they ever be a part of uncertainties of teaching twenty-five or more students how to read, write, compute, and think well. The term educators should be using is *responsibility*. *Accountability* implies that supervisors and employees guarantee, will be held accountable for, implementing certain methods in certain ways resulting in certain outcomes within certain times. *Responsibility* implies that administrators and teachers create the organizational configurations, staff development opportunities, and acquisition of materials to support an agreed upon instructional worldview—a coherent response to the fundamental questions of schooling (How do children learn? What knowledge is of most worth? How should subject matter be organized? How should we teach? How should we assess what students understand?). Entering conversations dominated by the fundamental questions of schooling returns professional educators to responsible discourses over how best to organize curriculum and instruction to draw out the interests, talents, and emotions of young people.

Second, school administrators must orchestrate a conversation about what is quality teaching. Our interviews with teachers about what they do in classrooms reveal that teachers envision patterns of instruction that closely align with research and best practice in the field, although the vision is often inconsistent with their actual practice. While the implementation of these patterns of instruction are complex and often are opposed to current institutional configurations of schooling, the outcomes of these conversations establish a common vocabulary or understanding of what is quality instruction. The shared understanding of what quality teaching is should inform much of the aligned business of schools: recruitment and hiring, induction, mentoring, certified staff evaluation, and professional development.

Third, school administrators and other school leaders must enter classrooms to observe the instructional truths in their buildings. The goal of these observations is to identify the depth and breadth of the existing gaps between the truths in the classrooms they supervise and an agreed upon instructional worldview. If school administrators feel they lack the expertise to conduct an instructional audit of their building, the responsible alternative is to seek out knowledgeable colleagues in the field and academia to assist with the important function of identifying the *what is* and *what ought to be* going on in a school's classrooms.

Finally, school administrators and teachers must work together to develop a plan for narrowing the gap between a school's instructional worldview and prevailing truths of what teachers are actually doing in classrooms. To flesh out this responsible plan further, we suggest that it should contain the following elements:

1. *Define quality teaching.* The foundation of school improvement is defining the criteria for effective teaching, identifying the gaps between that definition and actual classroom performance, and providing teachers with quality staff development programs that close the gap between what teachers are doing in classrooms and what they should be doing in classrooms. The research on effective teaching provides us with long lists of effective teaching behaviors; however, these lists of behaviors are often transformed into incoherent catalogues of teaching behaviors pasted onto teacher evaluation plans. A meaningful strategy for developing quality teaching in schools requires a process in which teachers and administrators author a model of instruction linking the activities of teaching with a deep understanding of how children learn. Responsible school leaders provide teachers with the materials, time, expertise, and organizational

configurations to construct an instructional worldview (recurring patterns of instructional practice) that dominates daily classroom instruction.

In conjunction with promoting coherent patterns of teaching, responsible school leaders develop and become partners in a purposeful approach to evaluating how quality teaching and a coherent curriculum are enacted. Continuous improvement in curriculum and instruction cannot occur in a vacuum, or for that matter, by analyzing mounds of data lodged in the main office. Teachers require knowledgeable feedback on how well they orchestrate subject matter content, instructional activities, and materials in pursuit of content goals. The feedback must come from trained observers and coaches who observe what teachers do in classrooms, examine what teachers hand out in classrooms, and review what students produce in classrooms.

2. *Take the measure of the current state of teaching.* In order to know what kind of staff development is required and the distance a faculty needs to move in improving the quality of teaching, it is important to take a baseline measure and take other measures at a later date to judge the effects of school-sponsored professional development. One of the many problems with the current accountability model is that administrators, and sometimes teachers, examine academic achievement data and must make inferences about the factors that might account for students' poor or strong showing. In other words, a principal or team of teachers might be looking at a summary of test scores and are left to *guess* why one group of students didn't learn much from instruction that has occurred *in the past.* Since we already know that quality teaching is the factor that has a tremendous impact on student learning and achievement, it makes sense to look for evidence of this factor. Of course, quality teaching is a rich amalgam of many behaviors and dispositions. A team of observers can find patterns of these behaviors and dispositions to judge where specifically a staff exhibits strengths and deficiencies and where they need support through professional development, mentoring, and coaching.

3. *Pursue a purposeful approach to staff development.* Another truth hidden in plain sight is the gap existing between theoretical constructs of effective teaching behaviors and a school's capacity to develop teacher understandings and applications of complex instructional strategies. Schools continue to address this gap with one-day workshops, weekend conferences, and summer curriculum writing projects. Teachers continue to respond to underdeveloped staff development programs with a variety of defensive reactions. The focus on underfunding of staff development programs has overshadowed the more important question—what constitutes a quality staff development program? Similar to teacher

evaluation programs, quality staff development programs must move away from indirect delivery of knowledge (guru on the stage) and skills to direct involvement with teachers as they wrestle with complex instructional strategies. Responsible school leaders design staff development experiences that include the following features:

- cultivating ongoing relationships with an expert/mentor who models, observes, and provides feedback on gaps between theory and practice
- offering continual opportunities to work with colleagues/experts on closing the gaps between the abstractions of policy documents/instructional theories and the realities of a teacher's classroom
- designing instructional venues where teachers learn the theories supporting ambitious teaching practices
- providing teachers with the flexibility to adapt the theories and practices of ambitious teaching practices to personal and situational conditions of their classrooms

4. *Promote a purposeful approach to instructional program coherence.* A given of the American curriculum, which includes the standards movement, is the habit of covering too much and understanding too little. On a daily basis in our schools, students are expected to make sense out of catalogues of names, definitions, and routines in specified units of time. Added on to this profusion of knowledge and skills are idiosyncratic efforts on the part of teachers to make sense out of these catalogues of knowledge and skills, all of which offers a recipe for incoherence. The only students who thrive in this instructional chaos we call the American curricula are ones who bring to the classroom an experiential background providing a context for these catalogues or a cognitive proclivity for imposing order on abstract symbol systems. Few students fall into either category.

The final component of a quality instructional program is a curriculum that is meaningful to the diverse populations coming through our school doors. What does a meaningful curriculum look like? It is not apparent in the mountains of materials sent out by textbook companies nor found in long lists of state or professional content standards. Meaningful curricula originate from the questions children ask and the stories that capture their attention. As children progress through the grades, these questions and stories evolve into common themes or problems aligned with disciplined ways of responding to situational problems. A coherent curriculum brings the full power of disciplinary theories, concepts, and principles to bear on questions young people ask and what they care most about. If pursued in a rigorous manner, constructing disciplinary pathways between the child and the curriculum and the school and society require teachers and administrators to look at knowledge and skills, not as discreet entities floating around each grade level, but as a spiral of themes, ideas, and concepts whose understandings are deepened at each grade level.

Bringing depth of understandings to the American curriculum, however, occurs only in classrooms where the criteria for effective teaching and how student understandings are assessed agree with how subject matter is selected and organized. Ultimately, for teachers and school administrators, the truth of promoting the intellectual growth of young people lies in a coherent approach to curriculum, instruction, and assessment founded on a deep understanding of how children learn (Newmann, Smith, Allensworth, & Bryk, 2001).

NEW DIRECTION

Our experience in observing in hundreds of classrooms and in examining the school improvement plans for dozens of schools has led us to some truths that have been hidden in plain sight before us. Here are some simple observations that must seem obvious to the reader:

- If students are going to learn and reach high levels of achievement, teachers have to teach, and teach well.
- Students' learning efforts must be situated in the context of a coherent curriculum, with the teacher expressing goals explicitly and linking these targets to previous learning and to subsequent activities and performances.
- School improvement and literacy growth and achievement depend on quality teaching *across the curriculum.* This means that an entire staff would have to share a common understanding of what quality teaching is, and the criteria for defining *quality* must underlie several aligned endeavors: recruiting, hiring, inducting, mentoring, coaching, evaluating, and training.
- In order to know how to improve the quality of teaching, someone must first take the measure of the current state of teaching in a school. The protocol for such an assessment should include direct classroom observations and interviews with students.
- Sustained staff development should focus on the areas of teaching that require growth. Our experience has indicated that most

often a staff requires help in making the curriculum coherent, in shifting the nature of classroom discourse away from recitation and toward authentic discussion, and in enhancing the assessment practices.

The decade of school reform has been dominated by the ideology of *accountability*—a strong belief in rational methods of analysis, cause and effect relationships, and extrinsic incentives. We don't see evidence that the emphasis on accountability and the proliferation of testing has significantly advanced the quality of teaching and the learning and achievement of students.

The theme of this book is apparently simple: If schools are going to realize significant improvement and advance the learning and quality of learners' experiences in the classroom, then attention must focus assiduously and persistently on helping teachers to refine their craft as teachers. In the balance of this book, we remind the reader that some pedagogical practices are better than others, we account for the environment that distracts school leaders from their core mission, and we suggest a rigorous plan for improving the quality of schools by advancing the quality of teaching. See the graphic at the end of each chapter for a summary of the plan and its recursive nature.

ARE THERE "BEST PRACTICES" IN TEACHING?

If we insist that the key to school improvement, advanced learning, and increased student achievement will come only by way of quality teaching, we should have in mind a conception of what quality teaching is. In some ways, it would seem relatively easy to offer a solid definition or vision of what quality teaching is, what it looks like, and what it sounds like. After all, students readily evaluate teachers in such forums as ratemyprofessor.com, and school board members from a variety of professional backgrounds express confidence that they can identify good teaching and that they know how to promote it. And, apparently, many writers judge themselves to be authorized to propose best practices for teaching. Using Google, our search for "best practices in teaching" resulted in 21.6 million hits. A similar search on Amazon yielded 792 titles. These links and titles on Google and Amazon offer both generic best practices that teachers of all sorts should honor, as well as context-specific best practices, such as how best to teach rhetoric and composition to first-year students at a community college. By the way, there is even a Best Practices High School in Chicago, although we are unfamiliar with the school's mascot. Apparently, a lot of people know what the best practices are for teaching.

BRINGING BEST PRACTICES TO SCALE

U.S. Secretary of Education Arne Duncan learned from his predecessor Paul Vallas in Chicago that a key to school reform is identifying best practices observable in the classrooms of a few teachers and then expanding those practices to a grander scale. This approach requires the adoption of teacher-proof curricula. The approach signals a surrender to a perception that there are weak teachers in a school and it is too much trouble to help them to grow or to try to get rid of them. Instead, the teacher-proof approach relies on highly scripted instructional materials and then monitors teachers through surprise inspections and checklists to prod the teachers to stay true to the script. Such teacher-proof systems arrive under the protective label of being "scientifically research-based," and managers of such programs insist that any variation from the script will compromise the "fidelity" of the approach.

On the surface, such a system seems to be common sense—find out what works and then hold everyone accountable for following the script. At the same time, academics don't agree about best practices. Even a cursory examination of several of the publications found through a Google or Amazon search will reveal that many of the claims about best practices contradict each other. This hardly seems possible if an understanding of best practices derives from a solid research base. Part of the problem, of course, is that scholars do not universally agree about what constitutes solid research practices and whether acceptable research practices were followed in conducting a study. Some authorities, including Marzano (2003, 2004) and Graham and Perrin (2007) come to their understanding through meta-analyses or other empirical means. Others like Daniels, Zemelman, and Hyde (2005) and Daniels and Bizar (2004) base their claims on observations and on reflection about their own teaching and the teaching of others over a number of years.

ARE SOME PRACTICES BETTER THAN OTHERS?

The question of whether or not anyone can say what best practices are with any degree of certainty is represented strikingly in a published debate between Peter Smagorinsky from the University of Georgia and George Hillocks Jr. from the University of Chicago. Smagorinsky (2009) insists that it is impossible to say for certain that there are best practices in teaching. Here is his reservation:

> A Vygotskian perspective suggests that the quality of instruction is dependent on the particular people who come together to teach and learn and the qualities of whatever precedes and surrounds them in the setting of the classroom. It further suggests that learners might have developed different kinds of worldviews and ways of thinking to motivate their schoolwork and that different teachers may be more skillful with one approach than with another due to their training, their dispositions, their experiences, and other factors. As a result, what works best for me in my classroom at my school might not work so well for you in yours. (p. 18)

In other words, according to Smagorinsky, all teaching is bound by a context. A problem with following a rigid routine or script for teaching—finding what works and taking it to scale—is that when real teachers work with real students in specific schools in specific communities, teachers have to make decisions about the match between goals, materials, and activities for a group of learners and reflect on the effect of decisions in order to inform further decisions. This decision-making process occurs in planning, from episode to episode or moment to moment during lessons and during reflection about the lessons.

In his response to Smagorinsky, Hillocks (2009a) agrees that the blind following of a script for teaching that someone has determined to be best practice strips teachers of appropriate decision-making autonomy. Hillocks agrees that it would be inappropriate to claim and follow best practices in the sense of routines to which practitioners conform. At the same time he offers this insight:

> If the teacher is the only one who counts in these matters, then perhaps one practice, method, or paradigm is no better than any other. But if the learning of students counts, then there can be no question that some methods, practices, and even paradigms are better than others. (p. 29)

In other words, if we are only concerned with the teacher's comfort in following a practice and with the maintenance of order and compliance in the classroom, then any teacher should be free to say what works for him or her. If, however, one is concerned with students' learning and achievement and with the quality of their experience in the classroom, we can learn much from research that tells us that some practices are better than others. Hillocks continues:

> Efficient reflective practice is dependent on being able to construct clear objectives and their criteria, to evaluate outcomes in terms of the criteria, to identify reasons for failures, and to invent better approaches to reach the objectives. None of this is likely to happen unless we, as a community of teachers, administrators, and university people concerned about teacher effectiveness, have a serious discussion about what English teachers need to know and unless that discussion, to borrow from President Obama's Election Day speech, empowers us to put our hands on the arc of history and bend it toward more fruitful practice in all of our classrooms. (p. 29)

Hillocks stresses the importance of knowing how to teach English well, but his observation applies to teachers and administrators generally. While there might not be a standard set of best practices that everyone should honor no matter the context, there are some practices and habits of thinking that are better than others.

THE POVERTY OF PRESCRIBING BEST PRACTICES

Even if we could say with absolute certainty what best practices are in every field of teaching, we doubt the wisdom of imposing on teachers and students a scripted system of instruction based on these practices. Csikszentmihalyi (1990, 2000) and Pink (2009) remind us that such an imposition would work counter to the forces that inspire good teachers to become exceptional teachers and would create a learning environment that emphasizes compliance over community. And if we care anything for the retention of good teachers, we should recognize from the work of Ingersoll and Smith (2003) and of McCann, Johannessen, and Ricca (2005) that the "stayers" are the ones who have a voice in the decision making in schools and who have a sense of their personal contribution to students' development.

Citing the work of Harlow (1950), Deci (1971), Deci, Koestner, and Ryan (2001), Pink (2009) reminds us that generally the tasks that people face in a workplace are of two kinds: *algorithmic* and *heuristic*. Doing jobs like repeatedly mounting circuit boards into television chassis as they pass on an assembly line would fall under the category of *algorithmic*, that is, repeatedly doing the same task in the same way. In managing a workforce that completes such jobs, it makes sense to monitor carefully and perhaps to offer some extrinsic inducements to complete the work quickly and accurately. In our view, the work of teachers is largely *heuristic,* requiring critical and creative thinking, and rational decision making from moment to moment, from a planning stage to a broader reflective stage. For such work, providing a script or prescribing a routine will actually undermine the quality of the teachers' efforts. Teachers need flexibility to make decisions that are most appropriate for their teaching context. They need a sense of efficacy in that they are continuously honing a craft, and they need an affirmation of the significance of their endeavor and its contribution to enriching a community and connecting them to it. In a similar way for students and for the work they do, they need some autonomy to make choices, a growing sense that they are developing significant skills and gaining significant knowledge, and a feeling of connectedness with others in similar circumstances.

While we eschew attempts to treat teachers like automatons who blindly follow someone else's prescription, we remain skeptical about claims that teachers should all follow the particular style that they decide works best for them. We judge, for example, that the style of a military drill sergeant who wants to strip his charges of personal esteem and individual identity in order to re-form the learners as elements in a cohesive unit is not a style that works for the primary grades in a public school. Clearly, we can exclude some practices as worse, even if we cannot specify a narrow definition of what is best. In the following chapter, we describe some teaching practices that we think distinguish high-quality teaching. More importantly, we suggest procedures for engaging a staff in the crucial conversations about what distinguishes exceptional teaching.

SUMMARY

In this chapter we report our observations from viewing hundreds of classrooms in a variety of schools. In our sample of schools, we have witnessed a recurring pattern of teacher presentations, student recitation, simple seatwork, narrow assessments, and relationships built on control. While these features seem to dominate, there is clear evidence that it is the quality of teaching that has the biggest impact on school improvement and on the quality of students' experiences in the classroom. Although we express some skepticism about claims about best practices in the sense of prescribed routines that remove decisions from teachers, we affirm that research reveals that some practices are clearly better than others. Furthermore, we insist that the path to consistently strong teaching will not follow from merit pay or the elimination of tenure. Instead, the process of improving instruction overall will require a common understanding about what good teaching looks like and sounds like, and a concerted effort to align several school efforts to promote good teaching.

QUESTIONS FOR DISCUSSION AND REFLECTION

1. As you recall the practices in the school with which you are familiar, characterize whether or not they match the descriptions that authors offer about the dominant practices in schools. What evidence do you see of distinctive and highly proficient teaching?

2. The authors express some skepticism about claims about best practices. At the same time, they insist that educators can identify with confidence what practices are better than others. Where do you stand in regard to the best practice debate? What features of instruction do you associate with best practices? Do you judge that every teacher should be in a position to follow any teaching "style" with which he or she feels most comfortable?

3. The authors presume to offer some truths hidden in plain view. To what extent do you embrace their observations as truths? If their observations can be taken as truths, how would you account for the difficulty in seeing the obvious?

4. The authors offer a seemingly simple plan for school improvement. But the plan might be simple only to the degree that it has few steps. What difficulties do you see with their plan? What leadership challenges does the plan present? How could school leaders overcome these challenges?

5. The authors claim to offer a new approach to school improvement and reform. In many ways, their approach may seem rudimentary. What, if anything, is new, and what makes the plan distinctive from the practices that are common in schools today?

ACTION STEPS FOR GETTING STARTED

→ Examine your school improvement plan to check that the high priority goals focus obviously on improving the quality of teaching across the school.

→ Meet with your instructional leadership to initiate a conversation about what quality teaching looks like, sounds like, and feels like.

→ Set a leadership agenda that focuses on the improvement of the quality of teaching as the highest priority.

→ Begin to fashion your communication with central office administrators to emphasize that advancing the quality of teaching is the focus for school improvement. The language of your communication should sound supportive of teachers and be consistent with the goals set by a superintendent and school board.

→ Examine the ability of organizational systems and the capacity of district resources to support a focus on quality teaching. Determine the changes that you might need to make to key systems and determine how resources might be redirected to emphasize teacher development.

Summary of Action Steps

IDENTIFY GAPS BETWEEN STANDARDS AND PERFORMANCES.

INITIATE or RENEW THE FOCUS ON THE QUALITY OF TEACHING.

DEFINE or REDEFINE *QUALITY TEACHING.*

ASSESS THE EFFECTS ON TEACHING PRACTICES AND ON STUDENT LEARNING.

HIGH-QUALITY TEACHING

MEASURE and/or REFLECT ON THE CURRENT STATE OF TEACHING.

SUPPORT GROWTH THROUGH TEACHER EVALUATION AND COACHING.

SET GOALS, BUILD ORGANIZATIONAL CAPACITY TO ALIGN EFFORTS.

SUPPORT GROWTH THROUGH A STRATEGIC PLAN OF PROFESSIONAL DEVELOPMENT.

PROVIDE MEANINGFUL SUPPORT FOR NEW HIRES.

What distinguishes **2** quality teaching?

T he previous chapter briefly reviews the debate about whether or not we can say with any certainty that there are best practices in teaching. While we eschew claims that there are universally recognized best routines for teaching, we judge that most experienced educators can view contrasting practitioners and say that one mode of teaching is better than another. The challenge as always in making a judgment about a question of value is to express the criteria that one is using to determine what is best. The following three vignettes invite the reader to identify instructional features that distinguish one teacher from another and ultimately to express a standard for recognizing high-quality teaching.

Teachers and administrators can turn to such authorities as Danielson (1996, 2007), Danielson and McGreal (2000), and Stronge (2007) to find detailed descriptions of the actions and dispositions involved in teaching. For example, within the framework of four domains, Danielson (2007) offers dozens of "components" and scores of "elements" (pp. 3–4). While we appreciate her attention to detail, we understand that most teachers and administrators need to rely on a much more succinct expression of what constitutes quality teaching. Educators need to know high-quality teaching when they see it, to have command of some viable language to describe the qualities that they value, and explain why they value these qualities. This chapter should help you to clarify your vision of what high-quality teaching is. This clarification is the centerpiece of what we see as the most hopeful school improvement or school reform effort, because a reliable vision of high-quality teaching serves as the overarching goal in a school that embraces the idea that *teaching matters most*. As we explore in subsequent chapters, a variety of efforts must align with a reliable vision of high-quality teaching.

THREE CLASSROOMS, THREE PRACTITIONERS

The three vignettes below represent three different teachers in action. The three teachers each take a distinct approach to the delivery of instruction. We judge that the reader can evaluate these three models and find the language to define the features that distinguish high-quality teaching.

Vignette

---

*At the beginning of his world history class, **Mr. Pavel** directed students to take out their structured note pages so that they could record the information that he presented about the Russian Revolution of 1917. When the students were ready to write, Mr. Pavel began to tell the narrative of events during World War I in Russia and in the rest of eastern Europe that contributed to the czar's abdication and the establishment of a revolutionary government. Mr. Pavel relied on a LCD projector to show slides of bulleted lists and occasional photographs to support his narration. He paused from time to time to emphasize what students should record in the structured formats that he had prepared for their note taking.*

In an effort to involve students in the lesson, Mr. Pavel posed questions from time to time. He asked, "When the Russian Army lost over three hundred thousand troops in combat during the first four months of the war, how would the public react?"

A student responded, "They would be upset."

Mr. Pavel probed further: "And when the military continued to lose thousands of troops in battles against a superior army, how would people feel when their military leaders rushed underprepared troops to the front?"

Student: "Upset?"

Mr. Pavel: "That's right. And when some troops were sent into battle without weapons, with the expectation that they would scavenge them from fallen comrades, how would the soldiers feel?"

Student: "They'd probably be scared and mad. I know I'd be pissed."

Mr. Pavel: "You mean you'd be angry, and you're right about that. When the people of Russia were short of basic food and fuel and everything at home was under the control of the czar's wife Alexandra, what would the reaction be? Would people be happy, or would they be very upset?"

Student: "Very upset."

Student: "I think that they would be like these Tea Party people we see today who don't like the way the government is run."

The comparison surprised Mr. Pavel, who judged that entertaining a discussion about the similarities would draw them away from his established plan. "That's an interesting comparison, Nick. Perhaps we can find time later in the term to talk about that. For now, you need to be writing down this information about the Russian Revolution. OK, so you can see that a lot of people in and out of the military were upset with the conditions and they wanted new leaders for the government and a more even sharing of resources. This allowed the Bolsheviks to gain more and more influence. Remember to write that down and check the spelling."

(Continued)

Mr. Pavel proceeded with his narrative and occasional prompting. He empha-sized those elements of the presentation that were likely to align most closely with the upcoming state assessment in social studies.

Ms. Beemans *hoped to expose her history students to an experience that would allow them to discover the stratification of medieval Chinese society. Although she worried that the sacrifice of instructional time might make it difficult for her to cover the target material for the first semester, she devoted two days to allow-ing students to learn and play the game of Chinese checkers. Ms. Beemans had recruited eight Chinese checkers "experts" from among her class. Each expert met with two other students to teach them how to play the game. After the pairs of students were sufficiently comfortable with the basic rules and strategies of the game, they faced off to play the game in earnest.*

At the beginning of the lesson on the next day, Ms. Beemans directed the students to take out their journals and write a one-paragraph response to the fol-lowing question: How does the game of Chinese checkers symbolically represent the stratification of medieval Chinese society? Ms. Beemans allowed the students ten minutes to record their observations. When she called on volunteers to report their observations, Ms. Beemans judged their responses to be uninformed and misguided. Exasperated, she berated the students. "What's the matter with you people? Don't you get it?" She then directed the students to take out their notes and record her observations as she dictated "Eight Characteristics of Medieval Chinese Society." When a few students grumbled, Ms. Beemans noted, "Hey, this is important! It's going to be on the test next week."

Ms. Parker *is inquisitive, and she hopes to instill an inquisitive spirit in her students. To her, the world is a series of puzzles to be solved. She knows that she can rely on textbooks to report how someone else had discovered something, yet the recall of someone else's discovery will not prepare a student to make discover-ies of her own. Ms. Parker also recognizes that discoveries are seldom haphazard or serendipitous. Discoveries involve purpose, method, observation, industry, and insight. Ms. Parker avoids having students memorize reports about the accom-plishments of others; instead, she creates situations where students discover prob-lems, attempt solutions, and reflect upon their attempts.*

In one representative lesson, Ms. Parker began her statistics class by reading aloud an article from the Washington Post. *The writer reported that a study sponsored by a perfume manufacturer indicated that there was a very strong cor-relation between the use of scents (for example, colognes, after shave, perfumes) and one's "sociability." The researchers defined sociability as one's inclination for positive social interactions, such as attending parties, going on dates, and gathering with friends. One's degree of sociability was defined by responses to a survey. The researchers calculated the correlation between the sociability score and the number of instances that a subject wore a scent during a typical week. The newspaper writer concluded the article by recommending that readers should "wear cologne, after shave, or perfume every day if you want to be popular and have many friends." Ms. Parker invited her students to comment on the article. For about ten minutes the students asked questions about the methodology of the research and disputed the writer's parting conclusion. Several students cited examples of persons they knew who never wore scents yet were very popular. Ms. Parker then asked, "How would we be able to investigate the value and meaning of the study?" Some students suggested that the class conduct a study of its own. "If we are going to conduct a similar study," said Ms. Parker, "we need to know something about correlations."*

Calling on volunteers for help, Ms. Parker explained what correlations are and described how to calculate them. Ms. Parker then used a small data set to model the calculation and determine the significance of the coefficient. She then organized the students into six groups and provided them with other data, such as a football team's rushing yardage and won-lost record. Each group calculated the correlation with the help of a scientific calculator and with Ms. Parker's guidance. In the next lesson, each group reported their findings to the rest of the class and explained whether one factor caused another. Other students from other groups questioned some of the conclusions, and the class worked toward clarifying their concept of correlation. Next, Ms. Parker asked each group to design its own experiment: "If the wearing of scents does not cause someone's popularity or influence personality, what does?"

As the lessons progressed, the students posed hypotheses, composed surveys, tested surveys, revised their surveys, collected data, and discussed their findings. The groups reported their study and findings to the rest of the class. In the end, each student wrote a letter to the writer of the Washington Post *article. In their letters, the students evaluated the value and methodology of the original study, commented on the reporter's conclusions, and explained their understanding of factors that shape personality and influence popularity.*

A SIMPLE TRUTH HIDDEN IN PLAIN VIEW

At the center of the policy debate over how to reform schools and improve student achievement is the seemingly simple question: What is quality teaching? While an obvious beginning point for any discussion about school improvement, it is a question that historically has remained submerged underneath other waves of reform initiatives that policy makers have found friendlier to centralized governmental responses to school improvement: implementation of governance structures to make schools more accountable; common content standards to make schools more rigorous; and charter schools to make schools more competitive.

Although each of these policy initiatives is appealing during an election cycle, none of these waves of policy-driven reforms has fundamentally changed the trajectory of student achievement in America. They have not altered the elemental routines of classroom instruction observed by Goodlad (1984) in his study of the instructional programs of thirteen high schools. This is what Goodlad and his assistants found:

> The teacher explaining or lecturing to the total class or a single student, occasionally asking questions requiring factual answers; the teacher, when not lecturing, observing or monitoring students working individually at their desks; students listening or appearing to listen to the teacher and occasionally responding to the teacher's questions; students working individually at their desks on reading or writing assignments; and all with little emotion, from interpersonal warmth to expressions of hostility. (p. 230)

Thirty years after the pronouncement that our *nation is at risk*, policy makers, state superintendents, and officials at the U.S. Department of Education are looking at recent research on school success models that articulate a simple truth: teaching matters most (Darling-Hammond, 2000; Wilson, Floden, & Ferrini-Mundy, 2001). Why has this simple truth, which appears to be so obvious to all, remained hidden from policy makers and kept at a distance by school administrators?

First, from an organizational standpoint teaching is considered a *coping profession* where the type of work is not observable and the outcomes are not observable (Wilson, 1989). Of course teachers can be observed, and test results can be analyzed. The dilemma for school administrators is establishing that important link between what teachers do in classrooms and what students achieve on tests. Administrators resolve this dilemma by managing the *forms* of schooling—scheduling, distributing curricula materials, employing consultants, organizing in-service days—rather than the *substance* of schooling—what teachers do with content, activities, and materials in the classroom. Recent reform initiatives have attempted to remedy the uncertain relationship between teaching and learning with policy formulations tying student test scores to individual teacher classrooms. Quality teaching in this paradigm of accountability is defined as how well a teacher prepares a student for a high-stakes test.

Second, embedded in this inability to establish causality between teaching and learning is a profession that has no control over the social, cultural, economic, and political variables that learning theorists and social scientists agree have a direct influence on how effective teachers will be in their classrooms. The last decade of school reform has paid little discussion to social context variables that policy makers claim are external (and irrelevant) to teaching and learning. When teachers and administrators ask critics to consider what children care about, what community they come from, and what resources they find in the classrooms they enter, policy makers often dismiss them as making excuses for not properly implementing scientific approaches to curriculum and instruction.

Third, for over a hundred years, Americans have been unable to agree on the goals of schooling. The struggle over the American curriculum (Kliebard, 1987) has generated waves of school reform initiatives drawing schools into contested battles over what knowledge is of most worth. School administrators and teachers find themselves caught in the ebb and flow of developing good citizens, graduating productive workers, educating intelligent consumers, preparing all students for college, and of course, making sure that tenth graders are scheduled for driver education.

In order to make sense out of a profession that has little control over inputs, that remains uncertain about what constitutes quality teaching, and that starts the year with new goals, school administrators and teachers have transformed teaching from an occupation characterized by creative, flexible, and intuitive responses to students into what Jackson (1968) terms the daily grind of schooling and classrooms dominated by "low task variety and low task uncertainty" (Rowan, 2000, p. 132). The assign-and-assess model of instruction works well in institutional settings designed solely to grant grades, credits, and diplomas (Labaree, 2000, p. 3). When the goals of schooling become focused on the forms of schooling (the granting of credentials) rather than the substance of schooling (helping students think well, write well, compute well), the question of quality of teaching is converted from what is *high-quality teaching* to what is *satisfactory teaching*.

High-Quality Teaching and Satisfactory Teaching

While a reflective reader might balk at this depiction, the reality is that a satisfactory teacher in an institutional setting is one whose behaviors can be rationally defined and, most importantly, can be quantified—measured in some way (Fenstermacher & Richardson, 2005). While remaining aware of standardized forms of reporting student achievement, high-quality teachers focus on content that is "appropriate and aimed at a worthy purpose" and methods of teaching that are "morally defensible" and "grounded in shared conceptions of reasonableness" (p. 189).

Satisfactory teachers are willing to adopt any method—test preparation programs, elimination of recess, retention—that achieves an intended learning outcome. High-quality teachers view teaching as a mutual relationship between the social and emotional responses of students and the pursuit of a valued end of schooling—level of thinking and methods of inquiry.

Satisfactory teaching, the search for scientific methods of instruction that link teaching behaviors with measurable student outcomes, has become the gold standard for defining quality teaching in America. From an accountability standpoint, satisfactory teaching (see Table 2.2) has all the characteristics of an effective policy: what teachers do in classrooms is observable, quantifiable, and reportable. Most importantly for policy makers, satisfactory teaching can be rewarded if successful, or punished if unsuccessful. While we use the term *satisfactory* to label a certain type of teaching, we do not want to suggest that this is the type to be emulated. It is a type of teaching that meets a minimal standard and protects a teacher's continued service, so it is satisfactory in that sense.

The observable problem with satisfactory teaching is that it looks awful in classrooms. Teaching methods and routines designed to be recorded (seven-step lesson plans, word walls, lesson plans on desk, pacing schedules, *I can* statements written on chalkboards) generate deadening instructional environments—teachers follow scripts and students are expected to replicate those scripts on a test or worksheet.

The real problem with a pursuit of satisfactory teaching is teaching methods and routines that fail to generate the kinds of world-class thinking sought after by policy makers and state and national educational administrators. No matter how divided progressives and traditional educators are on curriculum and instruction, all agree that teachers should be pursuing 21st century thinking skills that require students "to reason, think creatively, to make decisions, and to solve problems" (U.S. Department of Labor, 1992, p. 3).

Placed in the context of standardized testing, students demonstrating proficiency in 21st century thinking skills should be attaining advanced levels on the National Assessment of Educational Progress (NAEP). Since the introduction of NAEP, few students in American schools have been able to orchestrate the knowledge and skills necessary to achieve at the advanced level; instead, most students in American schools have stagnated at the basic level.

The fatal flaw of satisfactory teaching is a model of instruction designed to replicate and associate facts and procedures, but one poorly suited for interpreting and applying knowledge to solve messy real-world problems. High-quality teaching, on the other hand, is an instructional model composed of materials, methods, and activities that have the potential for placing teachers and students into activity structures requiring advanced levels of thinking and problem solving (see Table 2.2). In classrooms with high-quality teachers, students experience the following:

- a lesson planned through a process beginning with this question: What ideas and experiences do my students bring to this classroom that relate to a key topic, theme, or big question?
- scenarios and prompts that draw students into complex, problem-based activities
- access to a variety of information sources to mediate learning
- activity structures that require students to engage in task-oriented dialogue
- teachers modeling how they think about a problem
- teachers continually prodding students to apply knowledge to authentic contexts, to explain ideas, interpret texts, predict phenomena, and construct arguments based on evidence
- teachers employing a variety of assessment strategies to understand how students' ideas are evolving and give feedback on the processes as well as the products of their thinking

In the three vignettes introduced at the beginning of this chapter, Ms. Parker is working hard at being a high-quality teacher. She organizes subject matter, materials, and activity structures to facilitate the understanding of mathematical relationships. She enters the lesson with an uncertainty of where student thinking will take her and the mathematical concepts she is teaching; and before, during, and after the lesson, she continues to ask herself the following questions (Windschitl, 2002):

- Is the problem meaningful?
- Is it important to the discipline?
- Is it complex enough?
- Does it relate to the theme under study?
- Does it require original thinking and interpretation or is it simply finding facts?
- Will the resolution of this problem help us to acquire concepts and principles fundamental to this theme of study? (p. 145)

Unfortunately, school administrators observing Ms. Parker's lesson in a school focused on being satisfactory would likely express concerns about the amount of time spent on one topic, about the lack of a clear outcomes for the lesson, about the meandering responses of students, about the lack of alignment with state standards, and about unclear relationships between the lesson and state testing instruments. School administrators in this same school would likely be much more comfortable with Mr. Pavel. Mr. Pavel might be dealing with a challenging group of students, but he continually refocused students on the lesson objective, which clearly aligned with a state learning objective written on the chalkboard, and he discouraged any discourse and investigation that took students into somewhat unpredictable territory. Some supervisors would also be pleased with the direct questioning of students about the facts transmitted in the presentation; the students would be expected to master much of the content for the state assessment. Supervisors would be impressed with how skillfully Mr. Pavel redirected students who attempted to distract the class from focusing on the lesson objective. From one narrow perspective, the school was fortunate to have satisfactory teachers like Mr. Pavel teaching grade levels that were subjects of the state assessment system.

DISJOINTED TEACHING

What about Ms. Beemans? In the classrooms we observed in many schools and describe in Chapter 1, there were few teachers with the content background, training, or creativity to orchestrate lessons that evidenced high-quality teaching. What we did observe were entire faculties falling on a continuum between the satisfactory teaching behaviors of Mr. Pavel to the disjointed teaching behaviors of Ms. Beemans. Wherever teachers find themselves on the continuum between Mr. Pavel and Ms. Beemans, all teachers on this continuum taught a variation of a lesson with the following common themes:

- *Students disappear in the classroom.* The social, emotional, and intellectual backgrounds of the students are not acknowledged when teachers are talking with students nor does the content of the lesson appear to make any connections with the student's prior understandings of the topics presented in class.
- *Lessons begin with an assignment.* Teachers spend the first few minutes of class explaining the assignment of the day, completing a worksheet, reading a passage in the textbook, reading a handout, viewing a media presentation, or taking notes. Teachers rarely review ideas or themes that were presented the day before, how these ideas and themes relate to the objective of today's class, and how these ideas and themes serve as the foundation for understanding a unit goal. Of course, being able to connect the

elements in the curriculum assumes that there is some coherence to the curriculum and that the teacher can represent the subject as a unified whole, not a collection of disconnected bits of information.

- *Teachers talk a lot; students listen a lot.* The dominant discourse pattern in the classrooms we observed is teacher talk: giving directions, redirecting off-task behavior, and transmitting information. When teachers do call on students, the questions typically required recall of previously learned facts or a version of "guess what is on the teacher's mind."

- *Information is presented in catalogue formats.* Information presented in class is organized in the form of lists, outlines, or charts. Teachers explain to students that they must first learn definitions, names, steps, locations, rules, and methods before they can achieve conceptual understandings of a subject. The catalogued information presented in class is never associated with formats—narratives, big questions, themes, and concepts—that provide a context for understanding relationships between declarative and procedural information. Without a context for organizing declarative or procedure knowledge, the goal of all lessons is to know everything presented in class and the textbook. Sitting in back of classrooms where the goal is presentation and recalling for definitions, facts, and procedures, a learner finds it difficult to discern how all the information written in the textbook, presented in PowerPoint slides, or on worksheets will result in deep conceptual understandings of a discipline or how the learner will apply this information to problems in the discipline. It is no surprise to us when we sit in classrooms where no relationship exists between information and knowledge and hear teachers continually lament the fact that their students do not perform well on essays, word problems, or any task requiring the application, interpretation, or evaluation of subject matter content.

- *Did you bring your textbook today?* Catalogues of information are stored in textbooks and a wide array of commercial products that come in boxes with the textbook—worksheets, PowerPower presentations, media presentations, outlines, test questions, sample lesson plans. Too often, classroom activities relate to a commercial product associated with a textbook. The teachers' persistent references to information in the textbook leaves students with the impression—a faulty impression—that the selection and organization of information in the textbook is the way disciplinary experts think about subject matter, and that all the information in the textbook is a truthful representation of a subject.

- *Remember, you have a test on Friday.* The daily presentation of information normally comes to an end on Friday with the ritualistic giving of a test. In the classrooms where we have observed most recently, the teacher-prepared test typically requires students to recall facts and procedures presented during the week. Raw scores on the test document how many correct facts and steps students recalled. The strong reliance on forced-choice testing instruments reflects a teacher's need to grade tests efficiently—most tests can be machine scored—and supports the belief that the tests are "objective." While it is true that the end of the week test can be graded quickly, what is problematic about these Friday tests is how objective they are, given that teacher-made tests are notoriously subjective and fail to assess the higher level thinking skills that the textbook listed as unit goals.

Disjointed teaching privileges teacher talk over discussion, worksheets over real-world assignments, information over knowledge, and tests over performances. It was no surprise in the disjointed classes we observed to see most students check out emotionally and intellectually from the planned instructional activities of the period. Nor was it surprising to observe and hear teachers in these same disjointed classrooms express frustration with the general state of education in America and the lack of engagement of students in their class.

WHY TEACHERS ARE FRUSTRATED

When teachers are asked to define *quality teaching,* they use a vocabulary, cite activities in their classroom, and talk about goals that reflect the qualities and values of high-quality teaching (see Table 2.1). When one observes these same classrooms, however, teachers do not behave as high-quality teachers, but as satisfactory teachers or disjointed teachers (see Table 2.2). Embedded is this discrepancy between what teachers say and what they really do in classrooms is a narrative that recounts a deep frustration with what they experience in their classrooms. Whether in the teacher's lounge or in responses to a formal prompt, teachers cite a myriad of examples of student disengagement with the learning activities presented in class and the ineffectiveness of the sanctions they employ to gain control over recalcitrant student bodies. Typically these narratives end with the "solution" to passive/oppositional/uninterested student bodies—the administration needs to hold students more responsible for learning.

"Get tough" solutions for student disengagement with the learning process assume that students are responding *abnormally* to good teaching. In fact, what our team observed in classroom after classroom were students responding *normally* to satisfactory or disjointed teaching. Students will not hand in assignments, complete homework, or pay attention to the teacher in classrooms when they must park at the classroom door their emotional need to be known, their social need to communicate, and their intellectual need to make sense out of their environment.

What our team observed in classroom after classroom were lessons designed to transmit large amounts of information in short periods of time; the textbook served this function well. The goal of each of these lessons was to pass a test at the end of the week or hand in an assignment at the end of the period. Teachers in these classrooms employed a technique of the day—for example, cooperative learning—and the motivational tools of institutional schooling—failing a test or loss of points—to engage students in their presentations. In each classroom, we observed teachers who believed a lesson was a success when a form of schooling such as a paper, a worksheet, or a test complied with a prescribed format and was handed in on time.

Rarely did our team observe the qualities of high-quality teaching listed in Table 2.1; nor did we observe classrooms where teachers designed lessons that evidenced the following elements:

- clear and appropriately challenging objectives, contextualized into coherent units of instruction
- a knowledge of learners and understanding and sensitivity about their needs
- a deep understanding of the subject being taught
- activity structures that engage students in demonstrations and problem-solving that prompt generative learning
- classroom discourse that involves all students in purposeful and positive interactions and that engage learners in the thinking processes that transfer to subsequent learning
- assessments that align with challenging goals and offer valid means for drawing inferences about the learners' proficiencies and growth

School administrators, acting under the same faulty assumption as teachers—that good teaching characterizes the instruction in their schools—respond to student passivity and oppositional behaviors by implementing organizational configurations and accountability systems that pay a lot of attention to the forms of schooling and little attention to the substance of classroom instruction. Instead of a school organization designed to optimize the qualities of high-quality teaching, school administrators become managers of rules designed to hold students accountable for responding *normally* to satisfactory or disjointed teaching.

Entrapped in a school system where individualities of students are disregarded, where subject matter remains in catalogue formats, and where valued ends of schooling are remote or meaningless, teachers are left with the technique of the day or the program of the year to bring some semblance of learning to their classrooms. As teachers testified to us in interviews, techniques last until November and programs disappear at the end of the school year. The comings and goings of techniques and programs mask a simple truth hidden in plain view—*quality teaching matters most.*

Table 2.1   Satisfactory Teaching, High-Quality Teaching, Disjointed Teaching

TEACHING QUALITIES	*Satisfactory Teaching*	*High-Quality Teaching*	*Disjointed Teaching*
Goals→Outcome	Tightly-coupled	Coupled	Loosely-coupled
Valued Outcomes	Mastery	Proficiency	Creativity
Decision Making	Rule-bound	Experience	Eclectic
Knowledge	Standardized	Interpreted	Constructed
Intelligences Valued	Intellectual	Social→emotional →intellectual	Emotional
Risks	Minimize	Calculate	Maximize
Valued Materials	Textbooks	Problems	Technique of the day; current events
Tasks-Assigned	Low variety	Reasonable variety	High variety/low variety
Tasks Outcomes	Predictable	Developmental	Unpredictable
Teaching	Routine	Reflective	Intuitive
School Outcomes	Credential/grade	Responsible citizen and productive worker	Meeting student needs

WHAT IS QUALITY TEACHING?

The search for quality teaching has been reduced to largely ideological disputes between policy makers who want results (satisfactory teachers) and educators who want to restore judgment and meaning to classrooms (high-quality teaching). Quality instruction is an amalgam, albeit an expert amalgam, of good teaching and satisfactory teaching. Taken to their extremes, disjointed teaching can look like Ms. Beemans's classroom: a mixture of activities and subject matter content in search of an objective; satisfactory teaching can look like Mr. Pavel classroom: subject matter content in search of a meaningful context. In both classrooms, students either lacked basic knowledge (definitions, facts, and methods) or disciplined patterns of understanding (theories, ideas, and concepts) to think and act upon an issue or problem intelligently. In all the classrooms we visited, our team observed a confused amalgam of high-quality teaching and satisfactory teaching—what we named *disjointed teaching.*

Table 2.2 summarizes the instructional moves of two traditions of pedagogy that have dominated the conversation over what is effective teaching. Both views of effective teaching offer a blend of empirical evidence, ideological beliefs, and institutional rationale for why their model of pedagogy should be adopted as the dominant model of teaching in American classrooms.

Without a firm or coherent empirical foundation for determining what is effective teaching, school faculties are drawn into an interpretative act—determining what theories and principles of learning will be employed to construct a coherent response to the fundamental questions of schooling (see the list below). A consistent response to these questions by a faculty provides a unified understanding of what teachers should be doing in classrooms and what students should be experiencing in classrooms. Faculties that are "guided by a common framework for curriculum, instruction, assessment, and learning climate" (Smith, Allensworth, Bryk, & Newmann, 2001, p. 297) over a sustained period of time create a learning environment best positioned to grow students emotionally, socially, and intellectually, in contrast to school environments characterized by disjointed approaches to teaching, learning, and school improvement.

What teaching behaviors would be included in this common instructional framework? Historically, classrooms in America have been dominated by variants of satisfactory teaching. The egg-crate organization of American schooling coupled with institutional focus on the forms of schooling (credits, grades, test scores) fit well with a transmission model of instruction. There is empirical evidence that presentational teaching

---

Fundamental Questions of Schooling

- How do children learn?
- What knowledge is of most worth?
- How should knowledge be organized?
- How should we assess what students understand?
- How should we teach?
- What is quality teaching?

---

behaviors can serve an important function in supporting student learning of declarative knowledge. Satisfactory teaching, however, does poorly with teaching interpretative skills—the kinds of 21st century thinking skills listed in school mission statements. Nor does satisfactory teaching possess the capacity to induce the kinds of student engagement with learning activities required for developing high levels of understanding and conceptualization or what Pink (2009) names heuristic tasks—tasks requiring individuals to experiment with possibilities and invent novel procedures.

If applicative and interpretative skills have become valued ends of schooling, then quality teaching in our schools would gravitate toward a strong emphasis on the elements of high-quality teaching while at the same time acknowledging the necessary dialectic between declarative/procedural knowledge and interpretative knowledge. In authoring a model of quality teaching based on what is good teaching, faculties should keep before them four principles of "authentic academic achievement" (Secada, Wehlage, & Newmann, 1995):

1. A sensitivity to "prior knowledge" of students

2. An emphasis on "in-depth understanding" rather than "superficial awareness"

3. Representing knowledge through "elaborated communication"

4. Providing students opportunities to demonstrate competence in work products that have value beyond conventional methods of assessing student achievement (p. 9)

OBSERVING HIGH-QUALITY TEACHING

In place of the disjointed teaching model our team observed in scores of classroom visitations, we were looking for a coherent representation of

Table 2.2   The Two Traditions of Pedagogy

Fundamental Question of Schooling	*Satisfactory Teaching*	*High-Quality Teaching*
HOW DO CHILDREN LEARN?	• Imitate • Possess	• Discover • Acquire
HOW SHOULD WE TEACH?	• Transmission • Proof/demonstration • Test • Present • Perform/evaluate • Reward/fix • Remediation • Advance • Possess "substantive" and "methodological expertise"	• Rhetorical • Cases/scenarios/stories • Problem based • Personal modeling (living exemplars of certain virtues or attitudes) • Discussion • Argumentation
WHAT KNOWLEDGE IS OF MOST WORTH?	• Factual/procedural • Identifiable in advanced of transmission • Reproduction/mirrored • Right or wrong; Accurate or inaccurate based on model in textbook • Science/mathematics	• Narratives that would demonstrate/exemplify virtues, character traits, interests, values • Liberal arts
HOW SHOULD SUBJECT MATTER BE ORGANIZED?	• Textbook	• Thematic • Interdisciplinary
HOW SHOULD WE ASSESS WHAT STUDENTS UNDERSTAND?	• Pretest and posttest • Content aligned with objectives • Objective results • Achievement tests	• Authentic assessments

Adapted from P. W. Jackson (1986). *The practice of teaching.* New York, NY: Teachers College Press.

the qualities and characteristics of good teaching (see Resource B). Five questions serve as a foundation for a coherent approach to high-quality teaching and guided our classroom observations:

1. Are the observed teaching behaviors appropriate for the objectives and the types of students in the classroom?

High-quality teaching reflects a match between the materials, activities, teaching methods, and the expressed outcomes of the lesson. If teachers state learning objectives consisting of higher level thinking skills, then the organization of content, learning activities, and teaching methods should provide the observer with a clear indication that by the end of the lesson, students will demonstrate in discussions, presentations, and written responses the kinds of behaviors reflecting the ability to find and organize information, conduct investigations, analyze and synthesize data, and apply learning to messy real-world problems.

The selection and organization of content reflect sensitivity to the development levels and learning background of the students in the class. Lesson activities and outcomes evidence a balance between challenge and skill level of students.

2. How did the teacher demonstrate to assist students with understanding and applying knowledge?

High-quality teaching strikes a balance between strategies for mastering basic skills and facts and structuring subject matter content that grows conceptual understandings of the disciplines. Embedded in these lessons are purposeful strategies for developing discipline specific problem solving skills.

3. How did the teacher demonstrate clarity of instruction?

High-quality teaching sets the stage for learning, focuses attention, and develops readiness. Lessons include an overview that establishes connections with prior learning and a summary that reinforces major points of the lesson. For example, new concepts are labeled and organized into graphic representations that assist students with seeing relationships between themes, ideas, and big questions.

4. How did the teacher demonstrate knowledge of subject matter?

High-quality teaching reflects a deep understanding of theories, principles, ideas, and concepts that govern a discipline. Deep understanding of subject matter content is apparent in lessons where a teacher provides multiple explanations, examples, and illustrations for a concept and is able to manipulate knowledge in ways that relate to a student's understandings or misunderstandings of a theory, idea, or concept. Embedded in lessons demonstrating deep understandings of subject matter are divergent questions that generate elaborated exchanges between students in the class.

5. How did the teacher create a caring classroom?

High-quality teachers create classrooms with a positive feeling tone. Students are treated with courtesy and respect and no student feels left out. The discourse patterns in caring classrooms evidence that students are provided opportunities to express their needs, feelings, and concerns. Caring classrooms create environments where differing abilities, talents, dispositions, and experiences enrich the learning experiences of all students in the classroom.

We spoke recently to a former colleague and classroom teacher who expressed with regret that she often fell short of the high standards of teaching that she had set for herself. We know her to be an exceptional teacher and reassured her that she was a distinguished instructor. Reflecting on our observations of scores of teachers in several schools, we noted that we would be satisfied, as an initial step, if most teachers lived up to a "good enough" standard. In the fields of psychology, counseling, and social work, therapists work with a definition of a "good enough parent"—that is, one who provides for the basic needs of a child and performs the rudimentary responsibilities for childcare. In a similar way, those who work with teachers to help them to advance their pedagogical skills can insist on some essential characteristics. As a framework for assessing the teaching of the three teachers featured in this chapter and as a summary of the discussion above, we offer this limited list of key factors in teaching that will advance learning and foster positive learning environments:

- The teacher knows students well, and the teacher's planning of learning experiences takes advantage of knowledge of the learners so that the teacher can construct the appropriate instructional scaffolding.
- The teacher protects the safety and dignity of all learners so that they feel comfortable and eager to participate in learning activities.
- The teacher explicitly identifies target outcomes and situates learning by noting how the previous learning activities have progressed to the current lesson and by projecting how the current learning experiences connect and prepare learners for subsequent learning, projects, and performances.
- The teacher's ability to situate learning implies that the teacher works with a coherent curriculum and that he or she can see the connections among various activities and materials and understands the principles that unify the curriculum around essential questions or broad concepts.
- Classroom discourse advances beyond dominant teacher talk. Learners engage with each other in purposeful conversations that support inquiry and involve them in practicing the procedures

that are important to the discipline and can transfer to new problem solving, thinking, and performance occasions.

- The teacher has constructed learning activities that align with the stated targets for learning and that have intellectual integrity. The idea is not simply to keep students active but to be engaged in learning experiences that help them to gain a deep understanding of the content, advance their communications skills, and learn procedures that they can apply in challenging real-world situations.
- The teacher has sequenced learning activities so that they follow in a logical order, building from simple to complex and from dependence on the teacher to more independent application. The logic to the sequence should support the teacher in making transitions from episode to episode within a lesson and in summarizing the learning before moving on to a subsequent phase.
- The teacher monitors learning and relies on assessments that align with the stated targets for learning and require more than simple recall of discrete bits of information.

We grant that for many teachers this will seem like a rudimentary list of pedagogical practices. But we have seen most of these elements missing from the many classrooms we have visited, and we offer that the teaching in most schools would advance dramatically if teachers moved consistently closer and closer to this standard. We recognize, at the same time, that the concept of quality teaching is not a static and wholly realized destination; instead, as with any ideal, it is a kind of unattainable goal to which we can all aspire, in hopes of moving closer without actually arriving.

INSTRUCTIONAL SYSTEMS

A theme of the report on Trends in International Mathematics and Science Study (TIMMS) is the documentation of qualitatively distinctive methods of teaching carried on by teachers in Japan, Germany, and the United States—what Hiebert and Stigler (1999) name "instructional systems" (p. 88). Not only do teachers in Japan, Germany, and the United States think differently about the fundamental questions of schooling, but the policy and organizational systems supporting these distinctly different approaches to teaching and learning are also different. Placing aside the diverse interpretations of quality teaching in each country, the important conclusion of the study is that no definition of quality teaching becomes normalized or improves without a system—policies, resources, and organizational configurations—that supports and grows a country's or faculty's response to the fundamental questions of schooling.

This chapter suggests several of the attributes that distinguish high-quality teaching. Attributes of high-quality teaching that have not been addressed in any detail in this chapter but distinguish high-quality teaching are *coherence* and *consistency*. Without an instructional infrastructure supporting a faculty's coherent and consistent understanding of high-quality teaching, school administrators and teachers deconstruct the meaning of high-quality teaching into disjointed or scripted approaches to instruction. In the remaining chapters of this book, we devote our attention to a description of the components of an "instructional system" (see Figure 2.1) that will provide the knowledge and organizational capacity to support and grow a coherent and consistent definition of high-quality teaching.

THE ROAD LESS TRAVELED

Before leaving this chapter, we need to acknowledge as candidly as possible that school administrators and faculties who decide to pursue a coherent and consistent approach to quality teaching are truly taking the "road less traveled" by contemporary school reformers. Asking a faculty to pursue "ambitious pedagogies" (Spillane & Jennings, 1997, p. 449)

Figure 2.1   Instructional System

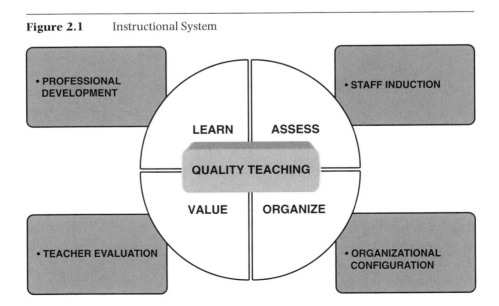

that are in opposition to deeply held beliefs and habits about what constitutes good teaching is a slow and complex undertaking. It is far easier to adopt a program, schedule an in-service session on the technique of the day, hand out boxes of commercially prepared materials, or direct teachers to comply with a procedural component of a state mandate.

School administrators who have the special fortitude and perseverance to journey on the school reform road least traveled—the regular presence of high-quality teaching in *all* classrooms—will be required to become proficient at the five tasks of strong instructional leadership:

1. Assisting faculties with AUTHORING a NEW LEVEL and MEANING for high-quality teaching

2. Aligning the GOALS and FUNCTIONS of systems (personnel, staff development, teacher evaluation) designed to advance the implementation of quality teaching

3. Protecting faculties from FOREIGN INSTRUCTIONAL WORLDVIEWS that endanger the principles, content, and methods of a school's interpretation of high-quality teaching

4. Gathering the necessary RESOURCES to generate the organizational capacity to support ambitious approaches to teaching and learning

5. Becoming an ACTIVE PARTICIPANT in the development and implementation of a coherent and consistent approach to high-quality teaching

SUMMARY

This chapter described three responses to the question, What is quality teaching? Successful schools promote a model of instruction promoting the transmission of large quantities of standardized content in scripted formats with the goal of doing well on a standardized test. Quality teaching in some schools is defined as improvement on limited numerical measures. We regret that satisfactory teaching is too often the acceptable standard in accountability-driven schools. Rarely do researchers come across quality teaching—classroom cultures designed around discourse patterns, activity structures, and subject matter that would arouse a student's need to be socially engaged, emotionally inspired, and intellectually challenged. The dominant teaching repertoire in our study of quality teaching was disjointed teaching—classroom cultures designed around disconnected presentations of catalogues of information lodged in the staid routines of teacher talk, recitations, seatwork, and testing of all kinds. While teaching that is disjointed might be considered satisfactory because it aligns well with the institutional goals of credentialing, grading, and testing, it is not designed to generate the levels of thinking and understanding called for in 21st century work environments. The ability to recall facts and procedures becomes antiquated in global economies that prize abstract thinking, solving nonroutine problems, and inventing new ways of seeing and participating in the world. The chapter suggests some components of high-quality teaching and urges school leaders to engage with others in envisioning a viable standard for excellent teaching, a standard that can guide several aligned efforts to improve the quality of instruction in the classroom.

QUESTIONS FOR DISCUSSION AND REFLECTION

1. The teaching vignettes at the beginning of Chapter 2 represent three models of teaching or what administrators and faculty might term *quality teaching*. Reflecting on the classrooms around you and the criteria used to evaluate the performance of teachers, construct a teaching vignette that would reflect what administrators and teachers believe is quality teaching in your school. Discuss this vision with others. To what extent do your peers share a common vision?

2. Decades of observations of classroom teaching in the United States document the dominant theme of disjointed teaching. From your experience in schools, why has it been so difficult for administrators and teachers to move from disjointed forms of teaching to good teaching that relies on a coherent curriculum and learning activities that connect and that students find engaging?

3. The institutional organization of schools in America and the emphasis on accountability have focused attention on the forms of schooling (grades, credentials, test scores) rather than the substance of schooling (what it means to be educated). In your school, what instructional activities reflect attention to the forms of schooling, and what activities reflect an attempt to address the substance of schooling?

4. Students develop deep understandings of subject matter when they are immersed in a coherent approach to curriculum and instruction over an extended period of time. As you think about the

instructional program in your building, what parts of the program are coherent and what parts of the program are more disjointed?

5. How would you respond to the five fundamental questions of schooling as they are represented in this chapter?

ACTION STEPS FOR GETTING STARTED

→ Teachers work at a grave disadvantage if they have to teach with a curriculum that lacks coherence. Take stock of the curriculum in your school, and seek assistance or initiate curriculum writing projects to transform catalogs of information into significant goals, connected themes or concepts, and learning activities that have intellectual merit.

→ Examine the assessments that teachers commonly rely on in your school. If they are almost all tasks that require the recitation or recognition of discrete bits of information, initiate assessment revisions that will present students with tasks that align with appropriately challenging goals.

→ Meet regularly with the instructional leaders in your school. Initially, the agenda for the meeting should focus on a discussion of what high-quality teaching is and the identification of specific instances of this kind of teaching in your school or elsewhere. Subsequent meetings should return to discussions of how your instructional leaders are providing the vision, support, and modeling to help all teachers to advance toward a high-quality standard.

Summary of Action Steps

IDENTIFY GAPS BETWEEN STANDARDS AND PERFORMANCES.

INITIATE or RENEW THE FOCUS ON THE QUALITY OF TEACHING.

ASSESS THE EFFECTS ON TEACHING PRACTICES AND ON STUDENT LEARNING.

DEFINE or REDEFINE *QUALITY TEACHING.*

HIGH-QUALITY TEACHING

MEASURE and/or REFLECT ON THE CURRENT STATE OF TEACHING.

SUPPORT GROWTH THROUGH TEACHER EVALUATION AND COACHING.

SET GOALS, BUILD ORGANIZATIONAL CAPACITY TO ALIGN EFFORTS.

SUPPORT GROWTH THROUGH A STRATEGIC PLAN OF PROFESSIONAL DEVELOPMENT.

PROVIDE MEANINGFUL SUPPORT FOR NEW HIRES.

How do we learn about the quality of our teaching? **3**

In the previous chapters, we make the case that the obvious and too often neglected route to school improvement and gains in student learning and achievement should come by way of advances in the quality of teaching across a school. Our hope lies with the teachers. While this might seem common sense to many educators and noneducators alike, we can appreciate that a principal who envisions the goal of improved quality in teaching across a school might feel like she is speaking a foreign language when proposing to a superintendent and to a school board a comprehensive plan for improving the quality of instruction. Someone might ask, "Where are our quality dashboards?" "Why aren't you data mining?" "What happened to curriculum mapping?" "Aren't we doing professional learning communities this year?" "Where's our technology plan?"

We see no harm in any of the efforts implied by the questions, and we recognize that a superintendent or school board member might have preferred projects and special enthusiasms. But we have to ask first how any of these efforts will significantly improve the quality of teaching. We recommend again that advancing the quality of teaching be the number 1 priority and that school leaders collaborate in aligning systems and efforts to support this goal. We understand that a vividly envisioned plan will not move forward without the support and encouragement of a superintendent and a school board. To put matters bluntly, a school leader will have to pitch the idea that the professional staff in a school and in a district office need to work in concert to advance the quality of teaching significantly and overall. Such a pitch should emphasize the key points listed below.

HOW TO MAKE THE CASE FOR AN EMPHASIS ON TEACHER QUALITY

- *The quality of teaching matters most.* To have a significant impact on enhancing students' learning, we have to assure the consistent quality of instruction (see, for example, Boyd, Lankford, Loeb, Rockoff, & Wyckoff, 2008; Clotfelter, Ladd, & Vigdor, 2007; Darling-Hammond, 2000; Darling-Hammond & Haselkorn, 2009).

- *High-quality teaching can overcome factors* of poverty, parents' education level, and other socio-economic predictors of school success (see, for example, *Achievement Gap Initiative Conference Report,* 2009; Boyd et al., 2008; Clotfelter et al., 2007).

- All systems in schools—for example, technology, assessment, curriculum mapping—should *serve the purpose of advancing the quality of instruction.*

- Research reveals the *pedagogical factors that most significantly impact* school learning (see, for example, Danielson, 2007; Marzano, 2003).

- It is possible to *engage a staff in defining the elements* that distinguish high-quality teaching and to raise these elements as the standard to guide instruction.

- The commonly embraced *standard for high-quality teaching should guide those leaders who are in a position to recruit and hire new teachers.*

- A school's *induction and mentor program should align* with the identified standards for high-quality teaching and work toward quickly integrating newcomers into the professional culture of the school.

- The *teacher evaluation system* should provide the protocols to assess rigorously the evidence of high-quality teaching and should *promote growth for everyone.*

- A *long-term professional development plan* should focus on the standard for high-quality teaching and support teachers' efforts to refine the skills that most impact student learning, achievement, and satisfaction.

- The *alignment of the efforts* listed above will likely *improve learning* and achievement significantly (see, for example, *Achievement Gap Initiative Conference Report,* 2009; Azinger & Baker, 2003).

- *Peripheral matters,* personal interests, and pet projects that distract from the core mission of the school to advance the learning and overall development of children *should not interfere* or compete against the concerted effort of a leadership team and teaching staff to improve teaching and learning.

THREE LEADERSHIP REQUIREMENTS

The central theme of this book is apparently simple—if schools are going to experience genuine reform and significant improvement, the administrators and other leaders in schools will have to focus on improving the quality of teaching, no matter how good they think the teaching is at the moment. In the long run, the quality of teaching matters most.

That's the simple solution to a perplexing challenge. As is the case with most worthy endeavors, the devil is in the details. Leaders in schools can make a huge difference by pushing the quality of teaching forward. But that's no easy task, we admit. In fact, the advancing of the quality of teaching across a school will require some essential leadership skills. In the last chapter of this book, we review candidly some of the realistic but not insurmountable challenges. We focus here on three core leadership qualities as a beginning point: *vision, integrity,* and *skillful communications.*

To begin at the beginning, someone in the school has to take the lead in envisioning that the whole school is going to improve and perhaps reform itself only if the quality of teaching improves significantly. We have conducted instructional audits in schools often enough to realize that the quality of teaching in any school has room for improvement. This is not to say that there are no distinguished teachers or that the teachers are incompetent or uncommitted. If anything, we have seen a lot of hardworking teachers, but an unevenness in the quality of instruction. We judge that the hope for schools lies with the teachers. But there is always room for improvement. We like to think of ourselves as good teachers; each semester, we collect reviews from our students and we strive to improve in the areas where students indicate that there is room for growth. We recognize further that we will never be perfect teachers, but we hope that the persistent striving toward an ideal standard will serve as a guarantee that students will enjoy quality instruction, even if it is not perfect.

The first requirement is a school leader's *vision* and commitment to support teachers in their striving toward improving their teaching, moving persistently closer to an ideal of quality instruction. But the vision does little good if the teachers and administrators in a school do not share the vision. There has to be a shared understanding among teachers and among various decision makers in a school about what high-quality teaching looks like, sounds like, and feels like. As we have emphasized in the previous chapter, this shared vision should guide recruitment, hiring, induction, mentoring, staff development, and evaluation. Here is where skillful *communication* and *integrity* come into play.

Of course, we don't think of communication in this context as simply a principal or other administrator telling everyone what quality teaching is and sharing the plan for attaining it. Communication is much more complex. Similar to the experience in the classroom, understanding derives from the various thinkers striving together to construct understanding. In actual operation, then, the process of constructing a shared understanding will require a rather involved conversation among staff about the need for high-quality teaching and about the criteria for defining high-quality teaching. Later in this chapter we suggest a process for facilitating a forum about envisioning high-quality teaching.

If a school leader has a vision for improving the quality of teaching and can engage staff in the extended and candid conversation that will lead to a shared vision of what quality teaching is, then the other leadership quality that comes into play is *integrity*. Simply put, integrity in this context means staying true to principles. A closely related concept is tenacity. The vision of a school that moves persistently toward an ideal of consistently high-quality teaching has little impact unless leaders in the school stay committed to the effort and refuse to compromise or rest in the effort. We worked with a school principal who impressed us by saying this:

> I am not going to let kids suffer with poor instruction because I was too tired or too lazy to do something about it. In the end, I am not going to let kids suffer if there is something I can do to prevent it.

This is an expression of the integrity and tenacity that are necessary to make a significant impact in a school.

The vision of improvement through advances in the quality of teaching and the understanding of the criteria for defining quality teaching cannot be housed exclusively with the principal or the superintendent. Teachers and other instructional personnel must also contribute to a vision of high-quality teaching and internalize the criteria that define it. Without the overt and candid conversations about what quality teaching is, there is the danger that various personnel in a school can have radically competing views, representing in the end a disjointed mixture of definitions. That mixture may be the worst-case scenario, but we have witnessed similar dissonance in schools where leaders have never talked openly about the characteristics that they value in distinguished teachers. An essential part of our vision for school improvement is that the various leaders, including teacher leaders, align their definition of high-quality teaching and work in collaborative harmony to convey the definition and promote the ideal among the professional staff.

DEFINING QUALITY TEACHING

A first step for a school leader is to engage others in formulating a set of criteria to define a standard for quality teaching. This set of criteria becomes the yardstick or evaluation framework against which to measure the current state of teaching in your school following the process described later in this chapter. If consistent high-quality teaching is the goal, everyone who impacts learning in the school needs to apprehend what that goal means. We can hear a skeptical veteran asking, "Why do we have to reinvent the wheel when there are several rubrics for measuring the quality of teaching?" Our response is that reinvention is a good thing, if that metaphor applies in this case, because it suggests renewal and purposeful action rather than unexamined routine. As teachers and administrators, we have had little faith in the idea that we can simply transmit knowledge to others. Even when we have expressed the requirements of an assignment with our usual clarity and eloquence, and students have nodded and smiled reassuringly, experience has suggested that there may not be a common understanding and we would never know the extent of students' understanding until we talked things out. Similarly, a school leader who wants to advance the quality of teaching in a school needs to talk about this concept with others. The leader might begin with a cadre of supervisors and teacher leaders and then expand the discussion to include the entire faculty. A more daring leader might plunge into the discussion directly with the entire teaching staff.

How could someone initiate discussion? There are many possibilities, but the facilitator must make what Martin Nystrand (1997) calls a dialogic move. A dialogic move would involve introducing doubt or providing the inquiry frame that would suggest that the effort involves shared inquiry rather than recitation of some discrete information. The way in which the facilitator frames the inquiry should signal that the discussion is indeed dialogic, open to multiple points of view, with the accompanying scrutiny of each contribution. As the conversation progresses, the facilitator has to prompt a variety of contributions, listen actively and carefully to each speaker, paraphrase fairly and accurately each contribution, and move the discussion toward consensus. This would not be a brainstorming session in which every contribution must be listed without judgment. It would be appropriate to ask contributors about the basis for their claims. Why would that be an important element in effective teaching? Can you cite any research or support from authorities in the field that would suggest that those are important elements in teaching and learning? While these questions challenge the contributors, they can be done respectfully and with encouragement. Some are more skilled than others in facilitating such a discussion. If after sincere reflection, a school leader recognizes that she or he is not skilled in facilitating such a forum, it would be appropriate to seek out someone from within the organization or from outside the school to help.

On different occasions, we have relied on different devices to prompt discussion. Sometimes, it is a simple matter of introducing the question, "What is quality teaching?" At other times, we have used surveys and scenarios to prompt discussions. In the resources section at the end of this book, we have provided a set of six vignettes that could serve a group as the focus for discussion (see Resource A). The vignettes describe teachers in action, and the descriptions will reveal a range of quality in the delivery of instruction.

The depiction of any of the teachers represents an episode in the broader experience of the teacher and students. But experience tells us that when a group of educators react to the models, they find ways to express the criteria that guided their judgments about each practitioner. A quick summary of the procedures appears below.

HOW TO ENGAGE SCHOOL PERSONNEL IN DEVISING A VISION OF QUALITY INSTRUCTION

The following descriptions outline a process for involving staff in discussing the concept of high-quality teaching and for working toward consensus in defining the performance standard:

- Set an agenda for the organized discussion: for example, "As a community of practitioners, we are going to express a standard that defines the priority elements in high quality teaching."
- Lay out the procedures for the forum: perhaps small groups will discuss first, followed by a large group discussion, while a recorder notes the observations and consensus.
- Distribute the vignettes or survey if these devices are used to start discussion. It also makes good sense to provide these ahead of time so that the participants have time to read and react.
- Organize small groups to allow everyone to have a voice in the discussion. Set a particular goal (for example, attempt to list at least five high-priority traits of high-quality teaching) and specify a time limit.

- Prompt the large group discussion by asking contributors to share the findings from each small group.
- Extend discussion by evaluating the lists of key traits and by adding to the list if necessary.
- Refine the list by asking participants to place the key traits in priority order.
- When the group has reached something like consensus, record and distribute the list of high-priority teaching behaviors to everyone. This might not be a perennial guiding document, but one that the staff can revisit and perhaps refine from year to year.

While a school leader as discussion facilitator will solicit and help to evaluate the ideas of others, the leader can also contribute ideas. We turn here to our summary from Chapter 2. We anticipate that a lively discussion about what constitutes high-quality teaching will include some of the observations listed below.

SOME RUDIMENTS OF QUALITY TEACHING

- The teacher knows students well, and the teacher's planning of learning experiences takes advantage of knowledge of the learners so that the teacher can construct the appropriate instructional scaffolding.
- The teacher protects the safety and dignity of all learners so that they feel comfortable and eager to participate in learning activities.
- The teacher explicitly identifies target outcomes and situates learning by noting how the previous learning activities have progressed to the current lesson and by projecting how the current learning experiences connect and prepare learners for subsequent learning, projects, and performances.
- The teacher's ability to situate learning implies that the teacher works with a coherent curriculum and that he or she can see the connections among various activities and materials and understands the principles that unify the curriculum around essential questions or broad concepts.
- Classroom discourse advances beyond dominant teacher talk. Learners engage with each other in purposeful conversations that support inquiry and involve them in practicing the procedures that are important to the discipline and can transfer to new problem solving, thinking, and performance occasions.

- The teacher has constructed learning activities that align with the stated targets for learning and that have intellectual integrity. The idea is not to keep students active, but to engage in learning experiences that help them to gain a deep understanding of the content, advance their communications skills, and learn procedures that they can apply in challenging real-world situations.

- The teacher has sequenced learning activities so that they follow in a logical order, building from simple to complex and from dependence on the teacher to more independent application. The logic to the sequence should support the teacher in making transitions from episode to episode within a lesson and in summarizing the learning before moving on to a subsequent phase.

- The teacher monitors learning and relies on assessments that align with the stated targets for learning and require more than simple recall of discrete bits of information.

THE IMPORTANCE OF CURRICULUM COHERENCE

We have listed above a set of key attributes that will distinguish quality teaching, but we must acknowledge that teachers will continue to have a difficult time in delivering meaningful instruction if the curriculum is disjointed. Marzano (2003) notes that one of the elements that make schools "work" is a "viable" curriculum (p. 22). One of the features that makes a curriculum viable is its cohesion, its representation as a unified whole, organized around concepts or themes that are central to the discipline. For example, a history teacher might convey to her students that the discipline of history involves inquiry into the way that various commentators have accounted for the events in history in order to assign responsibility and to connect causes and effects. That is a vision of a discipline as a whole, as opposed to recalling information in order to tell the story of events as endorsed by a textbook. We have spent a lot of time in classrooms observing beginning teachers, and we can report that the beginners struggle mightily when they cannot see connections among the parts of the curriculum and cannot represent any subject as a meaningful whole. Picture the health teacher exhorting her students to memorize a list of technical vocabulary outside of any application or discernible purpose. Or a math teacher who directs students to follow the same algorithm repeatedly with new sets of numbers, or the English teacher who has students complete worksheets to distinguish adjectives from adverbs. Imagine asking each teacher, "Why do students have to do this?" You can bet that students will ask this question themselves, and some will actually blurt it out in class.

The teacher better have a more thoughtful response than "because it's in the book," or "because everyone should know this," or "because you need the practice," or "because I told you to." Good answers to such questions are complex and they connect the learning of the moment to the essential question, big ideas, or themes that distinguish the discipline.

It is reasonable to expect students to want to be grounded in their learning—to want to know how we got to this point in our study and where it will lead us. Each day, every teacher should be able to tell this curriculum narrative so that students have a context for their learning and can have some appreciation for the significance of their study because it leads to a clear and connected outcome, product, or performance. If the reader labors in a school without a coherent curriculum, perhaps this is the time to excuse yourself to work on curriculum development. The teaching traits that we just discussed depend on it. Creating a positive learning environment, engaging learners actively in meaningful and intellectually valuable experiences, promoting authentic discussion and genuine inquiry, setting appropriately challenging learning goals, and designing valid and aligned assessment procedures are a few examples. Teachers who function with a coherent curriculum are at a distinct advantage because when kids ask, "Why are we doing this?" the teacher will have a satisfactory answer.

LEARNING FROM STUDENTS

So far we have made the case that a coherent curriculum is vital, and teachers will serve students well if they follow the instructional practices that research reveals will lead to high levels of learning, achievement, and satisfaction. Later in this chapter, we describe a formal process for evaluating the current state of the overall quality of teaching in a school. But an informal approach that both school leaders and teachers can take is to talk to students about their experience in school in general and in individual classrooms. General formulas for effective instruction are meaningless unless they work with a specific instructional context, with specific students, each with his or her own rich profile. Much like an orator sizes up the needs and interests of a specific audience in preparation for a speech or like a coach plans film day comments for a team, a teacher must determine the needs of the students to promote active learning, to display genuine sensitivity, and to maintain a nurturing classroom environment. That should sound familiar. The idea is that the practices suggested by theory and research need to actually work in application with a specific group of students in a specific learning environment. But what do teachers really need to know about their students? What information about each student is critical? How do teachers build genuine and trusting relationships with their students? What do students desire or expect from the teacher? How much can the students reveal about themselves and about how school is working for them and where is that professional line and that professional responsibility for the teacher? With school calendars packed and budgets tight and demands on teachers and administrators growing, figuring out how school is working for kids is often left to chance. Those kids who can make it without much struggle are appreciated and relished and those who cannot are, at best, left to fend for themselves. And for the latter, the history of their difficult schooling repeats itself. Without attention to the profiles and needs of the specific students in a school, the educational experience for all will be lackluster and unmemorable. It is probable that all students will learn something, but not as much as they could if all teachers had a working knowledge of the learners in the classrooms.

The simple truth is that all students, regardless of their ability to succeed in school, have both general and specific needs, many of which are never known by the teacher. If teachers take the time to pay genuine attention to learners, however subtle the message, their voices can reveal valuable details that can educate teachers about how to connect and engage with learners in a way that can be exhilarating for everyone. Students can give teachers insight on what works best for them in a learning environment and what gaps exist for them as a student in any given class. Teachers can quickly learn what makes their students tick and what is working and or not working for them in the classroom. Students often hold the key to better teaching if teachers take the time to listen, reflect on what they hear, and make changes in how they teach and interact with students.

Even today, with schools claiming to follow professional learning community models, teachers continue to function in isolation. How a teacher teaches is most often constructed without much input from others, particularly the students. They most often teach like they prefer to learn and how they have been taught in their own educational experience. This works only if the models they draw from were exemplary and if all students learned the way the teacher prefers to learn. Students' reactions to instruction from day to day offer a reliable barometer to reveal how instruction is working for them.

Another concern, and one that is difficult to admit, is that teachers come to the classroom with their own set of needs, opinions, and prejudices. They bring to the classroom their identities and needs as human beings. We can imagine that there has occasionally been a teacher who has previewed a roster or has looked at the faces of his students on the first day of class and expressed gratitude that there were only a few students with special needs or that the family of a challenging student did move out of district after all or that the ethnic mix was less diverse than expected. Fortunately, some teachers might privately entertain these thoughts and then rise to the occasion of being there for all the students. Some aversions that teachers have are natural. It is hard to find patience with the student who is argumentative on a daily basis. It is frustrating to have so few homework assignments returned and maddening when one reluctant student has yet one more unexcused absence from class. It is heart wrenching to know that there are students who live in squalor or whose parents are struggling financially. It is time consuming to prepare differentiated materials for those who need them. It is difficult to maintain a high level of energy in the classroom when teachers have personal or family commitments that require their attention. Any of these factors make the career of teaching harder than other service careers because teachers have a daily audience that doesn't go away when they hang up the phone or leave a meeting. Any of these factors, and many others, can rob a teacher of the desire or time to add knowledge of students to their already busy day. Any of these factors make building relationships with the students difficult. Knowing more could mean doing things differently. Knowing more can also mean that what a teacher does in the classroom will work.

In our experience, it was not uncommon to hear teachers indicate that their most difficult job challenge was the students who might resist the classroom expectations, fail to complete homework, and openly express lack of interest in the subject matter. Sometimes teachers have expressed difficulty finding the time to address those student needs about which they DID know. To take the time to gain more knowledge of their students would only add more to their already full plates. A desire to teach as much content as possible in what always seemed to be too little time exacerbated frustration. They assumed that more was better and held out hope that the more information that was given, the better likelihood that some things would stick and students would leave their class with at least some basic subject knowledge. Slowly the stratification of the classroom forms—those that can and those who can't, won't, or don't. The ineffective cycle perpetuates, but the teacher forges ahead in planning the next lesson, which looks curiously like the lessons from the previous days.

So, now what? Ironically, as we looked back on our collective experience of talking to teachers and students about augmenting classroom experiences for all involved, the teachers offered questions, the students offered some answers. We heard from the students that they do come to school with an idea of what it should be like or could be like. This is what

Gee (2007) calls a *cultural model* (p. 145), a brief narrative about the way things work, or about the way they should work. Regardless of their abilities or issues, in general, students have an expectation of learning, of being treated respectfully, and of enjoying their time in school. They want their opinions to be valued and their efforts to be acknowledged. They want to be appreciated for who they are. While they may resist or ignore adult intervention or suggestions, they expect to be made to tow the line and to develop skills that will serve them well as they move into adulthood. They judge pretty quickly who the good and bad teachers are, and decide what this means. They can identify those classes that they enjoy and explain in their own terms why they enjoy them. They can articulate what they would change to make a classroom experience better and what they would do differently if they were in charge. When teachers are open to hearing what their students have to say, they can make adjustments in how they approach their daily routines that will make a difference.

The importance of soliciting information and feedback from students goes well beyond the collection of more data. The mere act of involving students in any part of their educational journey has far reaching implications in students' performance, their accountability, and their desire to be successful in school. Too often teachers think that students don't really think about school in a critical way. They view their students as social beings who endure each class period to a given extent, entertaining many thoughts of the socializing that will come when the bell rings. While we know that students would likely rank spending time with friends in the hall above most classes, the authors suggest that, generally speaking, when students are asked honest questions, they will offer candid and insightful perspectives about their school experience. Generally speaking, students can offer two cultural models: a description of how a school works, and a description of how it *should* work. School leaders should pay attention to both models.

Students develop opinions about school and their teachers often and as early as the first day of class. They can sense whether or not a class will work for them, if it will be enjoyable, and if they will have a chance to succeed. If you have doubts, give any seven-year-old the opportunity to be the teacher for five minutes and every mannerism and frequently used phrase exhibited by that teacher will be accurately reproduced. This performance can reveal a candid snapshot of a day in that class.

So if students have opinions about their school experiences and can offer lucid insights, what do they expect or desire in the classroom? What do they say engages them or alienates or distresses them? What do they offer as the school experiences that inspire them? What interactions are found in those classrooms that create an atmosphere of safety, a sense of belonging, and a boost to their self-esteem? In our experience of asking students about their school life, both formally and informally, we have heard much of the same from all students. From those who excelled in enriched classes to those who struggled in special programs, what is commonly considered best practice in the world of teaching was often what they described, although not exactly in the same language that teachers and administrators would use. To give you a glimpse of what students have told us that they hope to experience in the classroom, we have listed typical comments below.

What Students Say They Want in Their Classes

- They want to be seen as individuals who could contribute their strengths to the vibrancy of the classroom.
- They want their opinions to be honored and to be taken seriously.
- They want teachers to have faith in them and their ability to be successful.
- They want an opportunity to trust and be trusted.
- They want to be a part of the planning and part of the reflection on how things in class and in school generally have transpired.
- They appreciate teachers who take the time to get to know them, who recognize their potential, and who give them an opportunity to reveal their strengths.
- They appreciate teachers who facilitate their learning by involving them in opportunities to think and share what they had learned—teachers who dignify their ideas and respectfully provide information that would perhaps augment or extend their way of thinking.

Positive Self-Beliefs

According to the students, when these experiences occurred in a classroom, they could conclude that the teacher cared for them, trusted in them, and was willing to help them be successful—simply put, having a sense of true belonging in a safe place that nurtured their self-esteem. This overarching theme was a critical affective component of the students' willingness to take ownership of their learning and their desire to learn. It was what they expected from their teachers as *the way it is supposed to be, the way school is supposed to feel.*

THE CURRENT STATE OF TEACHING IN YOUR SCHOOL

Several authorities suggest systems for taking the measure of the instruction across a school, department, or district. Valentine (2005) has constructed instructional practice inventories, and Kachur, Stout, and Edwards (2010), Richardson (2001), and others have drawn from Valentine to prescribe systems to reveal such elements as student engagement, questioning strategies, or technology integration. We defer to their expertise in the use of checklist systems for collecting data to reveal patterns of instruction. We describe below a more holistic system and offer the related probes in Resource C.

We recommend that taking the measure of the current state of teaching in a school will involve many direct classroom observations, interviews with teachers, and interviews with students. As part of the planning for classroom observations, observers must have a standard observation framework, preferably derived from the process described earlier in this chapter. A sample of such a framework appears in Resource B of this book.

For most schools of moderate size, we recommend that a team of three observers participate in the study. For larger schools (those over three thousand students), it would make sense for a team of four or more observers to tackle the task. To be candid with the readers and with the teachers in their schools, it would be a rare school that does not reveal room for significant growth. That's the point of this effort.

Here, then, in summary fashion, is a protocol for collecting data to evaluate the quality of teaching in a school.

HOW TO EVALUATE THE QUALITY OF TEACHING IN YOUR SCHOOL

- A team of observers observes as many classes as possible, across the school, in all subjects, over a two or three day process. Each observer does the following:
  - Makes a series of fifteen-minute classroom observations, using a standard observation framework
  - Takes extensive field notes during each occasion
  - Focuses on the key indicators of quality instruction
  - Attends to multiple areas that affect learning: for example, technology use, engagement, discourse patterns, assessment, etc.
  - Shares and combines observation data with team members to reveal patterns of strengths and areas for growth
- The team of observers schedules forums with groups of students. This is most appropriate for upper elementary, middle school, and high school. The groups across the forums should include all

grades and represent the diversity of the school. We offer a sample set of prompts in Resource C in the resources section.

The focus should be on students' understanding of when instruction works for them and when it fails them. We recommend that the facilitator insist that no teachers be identified by name, and it would be a good idea to include a faculty member in the forums as a measure of reassurance that administrators are not on a witch hunt. The facilitator should take extensive notes about the students' remarks.

- Facilitators schedule and conduct a series of interviews with teachers. In Resource D of this book, we offer a sample set of questions to guide the interviews. The focus should be on the way that the teachers represent their subject and describe how they teach a subject and assess learning.

- The team of observers and facilitators should meet for an extended period of time, perhaps a morning or afternoon or a full day, to share the data that they have collected. This process requires that each participant note patterns related to the key elements in the observation framework. The observations of students and the comments from teachers should serve to affirm the patterns and offer illustrations of the general patterns. The team should focus on the recurring themes in the patterns that the participants describe.

- At the end of the process, a recorder should note the areas of agreement about observed patterns of strength and areas for growth. Although the team will not have a quantitative summary of the patterns, the recorded summary of recurring patterns will serve as a baseline measure of the current state of teaching in a school.

- The team of observers/facilitators should be prepared to follow the same process again, after the staff and leadership in a school have had a chance to affect change in the quality of teaching.

- In the appropriate faculty forum, a leader should share the results of the assessment. Again, the point would not be to reveal particularly weak teachers, if there are any, but to reveal the broader pattern of strengths and areas for growth. This attempt at transparency should enable a school to set goals for improvement in specific areas of instruction.

We understand that the process that we describe above will look similar to the procedures that a team of consultants might follow as part of the accreditation of a school. If a district's budget would allow, it might be easiest for a school to rely on a team of outside consultants to complete the assessment process. Presumably, a carefully selected team of outsiders can be objective in the assessment and will not have a personal agenda, which can be reassuring for a skeptical staff.

This chapter has emphasized a process for defining high-quality teaching and for assessing, through informal and formal means, the current state of teaching in a school. The point of these efforts to define a standard and to take a baseline measure of the quality of teaching in a school is to set targets for improvement and to have a starting point against which to measure change. The related steps described in the following chapters rely on careful execution of these initial steps.

SUMMARY

The effort to improve schools, advance learning and achievement, and increase student satisfaction must focus relentlessly on a mission to improve the quality of teaching. This chapter describes the critical role of school leaders in implementing that effort and outlines a process for defining quality teaching and for measuring the extent to which a school measures up to the standard. We recognize that a school principal or other building leader might have to make this case to a skeptical superintendent or school board. This chapter provides some guidelines for making a compelling argument. We suggest that the framework that emerges from a collaborative effort to define quality teaching will guide a process of assessment of the current state of teaching in a school. We recommend qualitative procedures that can reveal patterns of instruction that can lead to the setting of an agenda for improvement. We encourage consultation with students to gauge the extent to which the teaching in a school works for all students and to find the immediate and commonsense ways to accommodate students reasonably to turn disaffection into tolerance and perhaps satisfaction. Throughout the chapter we refer to the instruments available in the resources section of the book to assist school leaders in facilitating discussion and in taking the measure of the quality of instruction in their school.

QUESTIONS FOR DISCUSSION AND REFLECTION

1. To what extent might the superintendent and school board in your district remain skeptical about a school improvement plan that emphasizes improvement in the quality of teaching in the school?

If they are likely to be skeptical, what is their alternative agenda? How would you shape your rationale in such a way that it does not portray a teaching staff as generally incompetent and emphasizes the common sense, urgency, and plan for improving the quality of teaching across a school?

2. It is easy to imagine that some teachers will resist an assessment of the quality of teaching in a school, and might express skepticism about the readiness and qualifications of observers to make judgments about what constitutes good teaching. What resistance might you encounter in your own school, and what steps could you take to ease the skepticism of staff members? How could you involve teacher leaders in the envisioning and assessment process?

3. How would you set an agenda and facilitate a forum for discussing the elements of quality teaching? Who would facilitate the discussion? Would you engage an entire staff as a large group or form discussion groups? What process will you follow to evaluate the contributions of participants? How will you come to consensus? To follow through, how will you elevate and communicate the standard to everyone's attention?

4. As an ongoing effort, how can leaders and the teaching staff become more attentive to the ways that students reveal the extent to which school works for them?

5. If you were to plan a process to measure the current quality of teaching in your school, who would you involve as observers and facilitators? Why would you select these participants? What training would you have to provide to ready them for the process of collecting and analyzing data? When would you initiate the process? How would you communicate to staff the purpose, procedures, and outcomes of the process?

ACTION STEPS FOR ASSESSING THE STATE OF TEACHING

→ Communicate with the superintendent and other district leaders about the importance of high-quality teaching and about your intention to follow a strategic plan to improve the quality of teaching schoolwide.

→ Plan, schedule, and facilitate a faculty forum where you will share your recognition of the teaching faculty as the key to school improvement and where together the staff will derive a set of criteria for defining high-quality teaching.

→ Plan a process for measuring the current state of teaching in your school.

→ Plan for an ongoing process for checking with a cross section of students about the extent to which school works or doesn't work for them.

Summary of Action Steps

IDENTIFY GAPS BETWEEN STANDARDS AND PERFORMANCES.

INITIATE or RENEW THE FOCUS ON THE QUALITY OF TEACHING.

DEFINE or REDEFINE *QUALITY TEACHING.*

MEASURE and/or REFLECT ON THE CURRENT STATE OF TEACHING.

SET GOALS, BUILD ORGANIZATIONAL CAPACITY TO ALIGN EFFORTS.

PROVIDE MEANINGFUL SUPPORT FOR NEW HIRES.

SUPPORT GROWTH THROUGH A STRATEGIC PLAN OF PROFESSIONAL DEVELOPMENT.

SUPPORT GROWTH THROUGH TEACHER EVALUATION AND COACHING.

ASSESS THE EFFECTS ON TEACHING PRACTICES AND ON STUDENT LEARNING.

HIGH-QUALITY TEACHING

What should induction and mentoring look like?

4

If a personnel director or other school representative recruits, interviews, and hires teachers, that school leader should seek to find evidence that the new hire has already demonstrated evidence of the kind of high-quality teaching that the professional community of that school values, or shows a capacity for learning the standard and for living up to it consistently. This standard should align with the efforts of mentors, supervisors, instructional coaches, and professional development providers. This process of hiring is a huge responsibility, requiring a certain aggressiveness, timeliness, tenacity, and integrity.

At the outset of a teaching assignment, it is both common and natural for a newly hired teacher to want to learn what is expected. If a principal or department head takes the time to offer a kind of orientation during an informal meeting, the new teacher might ask explicitly, "What are your expectations for a teacher in your school?" The more reflective teachers have actually asked us this question during interviews and during initial conversations. The school leader should be prepared to answer clearly, succinctly, and unequivocally.

As we have suggested in the previous chapter, the criteria for distinguishing high-quality teaching should derive from the extended conversation with the professional teaching staff. For us, in an orientation session with a teacher new to a school, we would emphasize the following:

- The teacher is able to represent the curriculum as a unified whole, with overarching concepts serving as the glue that connects all of the parts.

- The teacher is able to explain in language that students can understand the connections among the elements of the curriculum.
- The teacher articulates appropriately challenging goals and situates the pursuit of those goals in the context of the broader plan for learning.
- The teacher does not dominate classroom talk but fosters a safe environment for the students to interact frequently and purposefully.
- The teacher plans highly engaging learning activities that have intellectual merit distinguished by their ability to promote deep understanding of concepts, by their involvement in learning generative procedures, and by their demands for complex communication. These learning activities must align obviously with explicitly stated learning targets.
- The teacher engages students in goal setting, monitors learning, and applies assessments that are appropriate for the targeted learning outcomes.

Perhaps a school leader will want more than the traits that we have listed above, including collaborative work with teams, regular communication with parents, and timely responsiveness to administrative directives. That's fine and well. But first and foremost, it is important to let a newly hired teacher know what is expected in the classroom. The expression of expectations should be specific and focused and not scattered in a long wish list. It would be a dysfunctional organization indeed that would recruit the best teachers available and then look for ways to find fault with them so that they can soon be dismissed. A logical and organizationally healthy theme for hiring, induction, and mentoring is that the school highly values quality teaching and will provide the supports necessary to advance this end.

The induction of a new teacher is likely to involve more than an orientation meeting with a principal or a department head, and it will require involvement in the broader professional development program as we describe in Chapter 5. The process of induction will also require the work with a committed mentor. We describe below the basic components of a mentor program and then highlight a set of critical junctures that teachers face. We focus attention for a mentor program on advancing the quality of teaching as rapidly as possible, and we encourage proactive efforts to help new teachers to make the professional decisions that will foster professional growth and support student learning, achievement, and satisfaction.

BASIC COMPONENTS OF A TEACHER MENTOR PROGRAM

We base the suggestions below on our work with mentor programs at high school districts and at a consolidated pre-K–12 district. We have learned from the results of mentor program evaluations that invited both the mentors and the protégés to evaluate their experience. These survey results revealed ways to improve mentor efforts to support the needs of teachers new to a school district. Each component reviewed below has a level of complexity that we cannot expand upon here. Book-length works by Pitton (2006) and Villani (2009), for example, provide detailed guidance for mentors. Instead, we briefly describe the critical components to honor in order to promote teacher retention and to *accelerate a move to teaching excellence.* We appreciate the efforts of mentors who serve as the welcome committee for the school, but we understand that mentoring has to be much more than leaving cut flowers on the new teacher's desk on Day 1 and helping the newcomers to find the mailboxes and faculty restroom. We focus on features of mentoring that tie to retention and professional growth.

If a school district already has a program for induction and mentoring, it is probably directed from a district office. The suggestions that follow invite you to evaluate the existing program and work with the current program directors to fine-tune what you already have. If there is no formal mentor program, the following outline provides a blueprint for establishing a meaningful program that can serve all schools in your district. We understand that this is a collaborative venture that will involve school principals, district leadership, and teacher leaders.

Recruiting and Selecting Mentors. School districts with effective mentor programs actively seek accomplished veteran staff members to serve as mentors. Several stakeholders should discuss and contribute to the construction of a profile of the kind of person who would serve as a mentor. Several sources (Lipton & Wellman, 2002; McCann, Johannessen, & Ricca, 2005; Rowley, 1999; Villani, 2009) suggest the kind of qualities to look for in a mentor. The mentor selection should result from deliberation among school leaders who know the applicants well. The following list of qualifications offers a sample profile of the typical mentor:

- demonstrated record as an exemplary teacher
- strong communication skills
- trustworthy and sensitive to obligations about confidentiality
- experienced with a similar teaching assignment
- easily accessible
- responsible

- empathic
- supportive
- open
- resourceful

It is useful not only for a school district to identify a list of essential criteria for selection, but also to agree on a process for negotiating compromises when all of the criteria cannot be met. For example, if the new hire is the only music teacher in your school and there doesn't appear to be anyone with music expertise on the staff, who should serve as the mentor and why? The situations will be unique to each school, and a team will need to figure out the guiding principles that will direct these kinds of decisions.

Matching Mentors With Protégés. Perhaps the most critical element in a mentor program is making the appropriate match between mentor and protégé. It is crucial both to have reasonable selection criteria and to honor the selection criteria as closely as possible. While informal mentoring relationships will evolve, there are some obvious dangers in encouraging new teachers to select their own mentors. First, if teachers are new to a school, it is difficult for them to know the veteran colleagues well enough initially to be able to make judgments about the appropriate fit. As time goes on, teachers will naturally gravitate toward certain colleagues and select their mentors and role models. In addition, when self-selection is an element of a formal program, there is the danger that the same few experienced teachers will be selected time and again and will have to bear the bulk of the mentoring responsibilities.

We can well imagine that sometimes the mentor assignment is not a good match. We judge that in some cases, it is better to have no mentor at all than to have a bad one. The quality of the match should be apparent early in the mentoring process, and adjustments can be made if necessary. We say more about this attention to the evaluation below.

Communicating Effectively. It is important to inform mentors and protégés as early as possible about their assignments and to encourage early and frequent communications between mentors and protégés. In addition, if staff members apply to be a mentor and are never assigned, it is reasonable for them to want to know why they were denied the opportunity to mentor. In those cases when a supervisor has serious reservations about assigning a veteran staff member as a mentor because the supervisor judges that the staff member has less than an "exemplary teaching record," the supervisor should meet with the applicant to identify areas for growth and set goals for improvement.

Training and Support. Generally, a school district cannot rely on enthusiastic helpers to operate intuitively to guide their mentor activities. To have the best effect, the leadership in a school district should provide standard training that aligns with the research about common concerns among beginning teachers and emphasizes a coaching model for the work that mentors will do with protégés. Some school districts have found it extremely helpful to provide a calendar of mentor/protégé activities to help mentors to anticipate critical topics and significant school events. It is also helpful to have follow-up meetings for the mentors during the course of the school year. The group meetings help to reassure the mentors that they are doing the right things. Mentors often find it is useful to hear stories and suggestions from others. In some ways, the meeting of mentors provides a support system.

Observations and Meetings. For most mentors and protégés, the opportunities for observations are useful, although sometimes difficult to schedule. Scheduled observations, with the accompanying planning and debriefing meetings, support the effort to influence new teachers to be more reflective, especially when conversations about teaching refer frequently to the school's common standard for high-quality teaching. The observations prove useful for both the protégés and the mentors. Protégés can gain valuable feedback about plans for instruction and about the actual execution of lessons. The observations need to be purposeful, allowing for the protégé to direct the focus for the observation and tying the observation to particular professional goals. Certainly it is valuable for the protégé to observe the mentor and engage in a reflective conversation about a lesson plan and the episode-by-episode decisions of the mentor who facilitated the lesson.

Regular meetings between protégés and mentors are very helpful and are at the core of the relationship. This is one reason it is important to have mentors who are accessible to their protégés. Regular meetings allow the partners to build rapport, which in turn cultivates the new teacher's confidence.

Documentation and Reflection. While the obligation to keep meeting logs and written reflections can feel tedious, the documentation might be required in particular states as part of the recognition of a school district's mentor program as part of a process that moves certified staff along tiers of certification. Too much emphasis on tedious paperwork, however, can discourage the partners and interfere with the more important work of coaching and supporting. If documentation is necessary, it should be kept to a minimum and take a form that protects the confidentiality of sensitive reflective statements.

Ongoing Evaluation. The evaluation of a mentor program is valuable in finding direction for improvement. The use of written reflections and surveys for mentors and protégés provides summative data to allow organizers to judge if anecdotal reports of triumphs and concerns are representative examples or rare exceptions. It is also valuable to devise a formative assessment procedure so that new teachers can alert a mentor program organizer when the mentor arrangement is not functioning effectively—for example, the mentor is not available to meet, the mentor is assuming an evaluator role, the mentor is generally not supportive. The assessment would have to allow the new teacher to seek help without further compromising the mentor-protégé relationship. This is a tricky action to accomplish. It requires trust in organizers or facilitators and the promise of discretely intervening to correct situations that are less than ideal.

FACING CRITICAL JUNCTURES TOGETHER

We eschew reliance on "teacher survival guides" that draw from the author's personal experience alone and disregard research about the actual concerns of beginning teachers and the support needed to foster their rapid development. We have looked for answers as to why apparently good beginning teachers "go bad," as one principal friend put it, and leave the profession, either on their own or at the urging of their supervisors. Our work with supervisors of teachers in all subjects and all grades, kindergarten through 12, suggests that as beginners advance into the profession, they face certain *critical junctures* when they can make good choices and grow in the profession, or make bad choices that will direct them down a less rewarding path. We define *critical junctures* here as moments of decision, sometimes recurring, that can significantly influence a teacher's sense of efficacy and affect retention. In short, we see some promise in mentors' anticipating these critical junctures and being equipped with the skills to coach the new teacher through them.

Again, we contrast our sense of critical junctures with the conventional wisdom we have seen offered in teacher survival guides. If we were to put our faith in the advice from popular survival guides, here would be the priorities:

- Don't smile before Thanksgiving. The sentiment is this—be stern and distant if you want students to respect you.
- Set rules, policies, and deadlines and follow them with iron-willed rigidity.

- Dress in "professional" attire in order to establish credibility with students, parents, colleagues, and supervisors.
- Maintain fresh and attractive bulletin boards that will inspire learners to master the content of a subject.
- Keep learners busy with lots of written work.

In contrast, our experience with supervisors of teachers reveals to us that the following are the more critical episodes, when the decisions that a teacher makes can lead to a constructive or destructive experience:

- What kind of relationship will you form with students? This is far and away the most important consideration.
- Who will you listen to for directions regarding pedagogy and policies? New teachers run into problems when they mistake eager advisers for reliable mentors.
- Who will be your informal mentors? The choice of mentors, role models, influences, and associates can define the quality of your experience.
- Will you ever get out of your room? Teaching can be an isolating experience unless you connect yourself and your efforts to the community of professionals who share a common goal.
- Can you recover from hurtful experiences? Inevitably, a critical or insensitive remark or action can be painful; recovering resiliently is the important consideration.
- Can you bounce back from mistakes? Perfection is tough to attain, but bouncing back from mistakes is within human capabilities.
- Can you be the teacher you were trained to be? Sometimes the culture or curriculum of a school or of a department works against one fitting into the teacher persona that training and early experience shaped.
- Can you choose routines that will help you stay well? We know what we are supposed to do to stay well; it is tough to treat ourselves with the care we need.

Although administrators are not quick to recognize it, we judge that another critical juncture occurs when a teacher is invited to participate in a workshop or conference or encouraged to join a professional organization. The affirmative choice connects the teacher to a larger professional community, which we think is crucial, but less valued by the supervisors we have interviewed.

Recognition of these critical junctures should direct supervisors and mentors to be proactive in anticipating when tough choices emerge and to be ready to assist in reflecting on the choices. Mentors should be equipped to coach new teachers through some tough choices and, in some instances, influence them toward the "better" choice, if *better* means more child-centered, optimistic, and constructive.

Learning about the actual experience of a new colleague is a first step, just as knowing about a class of learners helps the teacher to plan instruction. Experience tells us to avoid presuming what difficulties early career teachers might be facing. Instead, it is wise to look at the patterns of experience that the research reveals and to inquire into the experience of a new colleague to find out what parts of the job bring joy and satisfaction and what parts cause distress. Equipped with some knowledge about the lives of beginners, a mentor can anticipate predictable experiences and be proactive in coaching a colleague. Again, we judge that any human fixates belief through a process of inquiry and discovery, not simply by being told what to do. And coaching involves a set of skills that we all need to learn and practice in order to help a colleague to reflect on options and make sound decisions.

Learning From Good Experienced Teachers

We appreciate mentors who are eager to make new teachers feel welcome and who seek to help the newcomers to adjust to new surroundings. We judge, however, that this initial focus on orientation to the school organization needs to shift quickly into an emphasis on how to perform as highly effective teachers. Our simple prescription for new teachers is to ignore the teacher survival guides and to look instead to the examples of highly effective, experienced teachers within your own school. Good experienced teachers are different from newly minted teachers, and we note some of these differences below.

New teachers who leave their teacher preparation programs with a solid theoretical base to guide their practice can draw from theory to say generally how they can plan instruction. In contrast, experienced teachers can envision their plans in great detail. Experienced teachers can search memory and evaluate several choices that they have available to them to contend with planning or problem solving. Veteran teachers benefit from recalling several possibilities from past experience in the classroom. Whether the situation involves a curriculum decision or other professional problem solving, experienced teachers can usually select an appropriate choice to fit the current situation. Experienced teachers often operate from a strong theoretical base to judge which possibilities are appropriate and which are best. But experienced teachers have more than theory because they draw from episodes from teaching experience to validate the direction that they are inclined to follow. Not only do the experienced teachers have options from which to choose for current action, they have several contingencies from which to draw in case the initial choice does not seem possible or current circumstances suggest a different direction.

In part, the choices available to experienced teachers come from an ability to *anticipate* possible outcomes and complications. They know what is likely to happen if they initiate a particular assignment or activity, introduce a particular problem or text, or propose specific writing. In essence, the seasoned practitioner reflects on the same or analogous situations from the past to predict how students are likely to respond. This capacity to anticipate outcomes allows the teacher to decide whether to go forward with plans or to alter them in some way. In addition, anticipating events allows the teacher to imagine contingencies in the event that lessons advance in any of several directions.

New teachers find it helpful to know the underlying principles that drive the curriculum. While it is helpful to have access to curriculum guides and classroom materials, teachers also need to know why other teachers have determined that students should pursue particular goals, read particular texts, and engage in particular activities. An understanding of the guiding principles for the courses or content they teach allows teachers to make decisions that provide for variations and creativity while remaining true to the central principles for the instruction. Having a clear *vision* of what one should teach and how to teach it, is a powerful benefit for day-to-day operation in the classroom. Typically, after years of practice and reflection, a strong, experienced teacher will have a solid vision of what the enterprise of teaching a particular subject is about, including a detailed image of what the teacher's role is and what the classroom dynamic should look like from day to day.

Experienced teachers have a further advantage of knowing much about the students, the community, the culture of the school and department, and the resources within the school. Without an *awareness* of features of the school organization, of common practices among colleagues, and of traditions in the school or profession, the new teachers' choices for action are limited. In planning instruction and in contending with any of a number of problem-solving situations, teachers have options when they are aware of resources, constraints, and possibilities. It is fairly common for a new teacher to observe how an experienced teacher has addressed a problem or planned some element in a unit of instruction and to note, "I didn't know that I could do that." The situations might include planning for assessment, replying to an angry parent, preparing for a classroom observation, or requesting to attend a professional conference.

The several advantages that come from experience—*choices, anticipation, vision,* and *awareness*—all contribute to a growing sense of *confidence.* Beginning teachers reveal that without confidence, they are often inhibited by the doubts they have about making decisions and about taking the actions that they feel intuitively inclined to take. Some people give the impression that they are innately confident, but confidence grows from having a solid sense of mission, from anticipating outcomes, from having choices, and from being aware of resources and options.

The Power of Collaboration

With schools required to follow a Response to Intervention (RTI) protocol and with many schools invested in the idea of a Professional Learning Community, the practice of collaboration among colleagues would seem to be commonplace in schools. Beyond the collegial discussions of assessment data and team planning for interventions for individual students, many other collaborative efforts can accelerate the development of a beginning teacher. Collaboration provides new teachers with many of the advantages that experienced teachers have.

After several years of observing teams of teachers who work in highly functional, collaborative groups in elementary schools, middle schools, and high schools, and other teachers who work in a more independent and isolated fashion, we can note several contrasts. Collaborative teams tend to plan strategically, keeping specific target outcomes in mind, and planning together a course of instruction that offers the strongest potential for students to attain goals. While teachers who plan in relative isolation work conscientiously, they are less inclined to express in detail the kind of learning they want to result from their instruction. In the planning and debriefing sessions, we have witnessed collaborative teams generating and assessing multiple options for lesson activities. With each team member bringing a different experience and a different wealth of knowledge to the task, collaborative teams drew from multiple resources for planning. This would be impossible, or at least limited, with the beginning teachers who work in a more isolated mode. When teams of teachers have met to debrief about the effects of instruction, they have used their insights about current instruction to advance the team planning. We have witnessed collaborative teams posing essential questions of each other. Here are two examples: "How will we know if the activities helped the students to understand what they read?" "How do we know the extent to which the class discussions prepared the students for writing analyses of their reading?" The questions prompted the discussion of an assessment plan that would allow the team to answer their questions.

Essentially, then, the collaborative team conducted action research. We have witnessed little evidence of such attempts among teachers who operate in a more isolated way.

So picture a team of teachers planning a unit of instruction together. They talk about their expectations for students' learning, including the quality of the students' experience in the classroom. As they plan the learning activities, they explore and evaluate several possibilities, with each participant offering suggestions. The suggestions draw from each participant's store of knowledge and take advantage of that teacher's strengths and interests. As they weigh the merits of the various options, they identify the resources they need to tap. They provide for the assessment of learning—in the near term, judging if students are learning concepts and procedures as predicted and in the long term, measuring growth over time.

Mentoring as a Team Effort

In the end, when new teachers join with capable, experienced colleagues in the planning and assessing of instruction, they function more like the veteran colleagues that they admire. A seemingly simple avenue to mentoring beginning teachers is to guide them to join regularly with a collaborative team. This recommendation presumes that such collaborative teams already exist in schools. If they do not, the first step is to invite colleagues to participate in group planning, problem solving, and assessing. Such teams do not emerge by chance, and they do not continue to work productively without attention. A mentor must assume leadership and facilitate discussions to encourage contributions, to affirm commitments, and to attend to follow-up obligations. In such a collaborative environment, mentoring means more than the one-on-one guidance between veteran and beginner; instead, mentoring is a group effort, involving practitioners with a variety of experience and providing an influential model for how colleagues work together as a matter of course.

PLANNING FOR NEW TEACHERS' SUCCESS

Too often, the school leaders who design the master schedule and decide the teaching assignments for new teachers assign the newcomers the most difficult schedules. The difficulty might include multiple preparations for classes with the neediest and most challenging students and moves to three or four different classrooms throughout the school day. These difficult assignments convey a regrettable view of new teachers as initiates who have to endure hardship in order to develop resiliency while earning a status that warrants a more humane experience. We find this view of new teachers as low status initiates disturbing, to say the least.

The appropriate approach and attitude involves planning for new teachers to become the highest quality teachers as soon as possible. Mentors have to support this effort by doing more than serving as the welcoming committee. They need to train to coach protégés to live up to the local standards for quality teaching and to prompt a reflective disposition to continue to grow and strive for consistently high-quality teaching.

SUMMARY

The initiation, organization, and management of a mentor program will be complicated, and the brief outline above highlights a few key considerations. In the end, new staff members need to know that at the center of the mentor program are people who are eager to help their colleagues and who have developed some skills for coaching others as they encounter challenges and as they grow as professionals. Beyond considering this brief review, teachers who are assuming leadership for a mentor program should look to the substantial body of literature about mentoring and look at any exemplary mentor program that they can identify. We urge careful preparation for the procedures and the training, because we have seen instances when no mentoring at all would have been better than the misguided mentoring that some beginning teachers have experienced. We also encourage school leaders to foster collaborative relationships so that mentoring can continue as a group effort.

QUESTIONS FOR DISCUSSION AND REFLECTION

1. Imagine that you have just hired a new teacher who asks, "What do you expect of your teachers?" How will you answer that question in a way that makes expectations explicit to new staff members?

2. Project how you would establish or refine a mentor program for your school. Which teachers can join in the planning? What qualities do these teachers bring to the effort? What qualities do you look for in mentors?

3. How would you devise a system for the selection and communication for mentors? How will you initiate the communication between mentor and protégé?

4. How will you provide for the assessment of a mentor program? How can you monitor the program so that you can make adjustments during the course of the school year?

5. How can you encourage collaborative planning and reflection among teams of teachers in your school? How would teams form? Who would assume leadership within the teams? How will you support the development of the leadership skills that are necessary to help teams function productively?

ACTION STEPS FOR INDUCTION AND MENTORING

→ Prepare a response to a new teacher who might ask, "What do you expect of your teachers?"

→ Work with the current mentor coordinator to help to refine key elements in the mentor program.

→ Plan professional development experiences that will help mentors and school supervisors to acquire and polish the coaching strategies that support mentoring efforts.

→ Foster collaborative groups and cooperative relationships among teams of teachers.

Source: This chapter draws from two previously-published articles.

McCann, T. M., & Johannessen, L. R. (2008). Defying conventional wisdom. *English Journal. (98)* 1, 90–92. Copyright 2008 by the National Council of Teachers of English. Reprinted with permission.

McCann, T. M. (2010). Designing a mentor program. *English Journal. (99)* 4, 94–96. Copyright 2010 by the National Council of Teachers of English. Reprinted with permission.

Summary of Action Steps

IDENTIFY GAPS BETWEEN STANDARDS AND PERFORMANCES.

INITIATE or RENEW THE FOCUS ON THE QUALITY OF TEACHING.

ASSESS THE EFFECTS ON TEACHING PRACTICES AND ON STUDENT LEARNING.

DEFINE or REDEFINE *QUALITY TEACHING.*

HIGH-QUALITY TEACHING

MEASURE and/or REFLECT ON THE CURRENT STATE OF TEACHING.

SUPPORT GROWTH THROUGH TEACHER EVALUATION AND COACHING.

SET GOALS, BUILD ORGANIZATIONAL CAPACITY TO ALIGN EFFORTS.

SUPPORT GROWTH THROUGH A STRATEGIC PLAN OF PROFESSIONAL DEVELOPMENT.

PROVIDE MEANINGFUL SUPPORT FOR NEW HIRES.

What should professional development look like?

5

In the last two chapters, we have recommended coordinated actions to recruit, induct, and mentor teachers to promote consistent high-quality teaching. We turn now to professional development, which potentially influences the practices of new and veteran teachers alike. As teachers for many years in a variety of schools, we know that poorly planned and weakly executed professional development can be routine and lackluster. We also know that professional development can be transformative. If professional development is to become something more than the dissemination of information about current mandates, it should be:

- focused on advancing the quality of teaching and learning
- representative of a long-term strategic plan
- collaboratively developed by teachers and administrators working in concert
- sustained and supported
- pursued through inquiry, application, and discovery, rather than through recall and routine practice

In this chapter we provide a rationale and a process for the planning and delivery of meaningful professional development that promotes high-quality teaching.

We have represented in Figure 5.1 the plan for an institute day at the prototypical Wood Knoll School District 582. Numerous studies of schools' attempts at staff development have documented the ineffectiveness of approaches like Wood Knoll's to educate and train staff in a selected technique. We offer this fictional example to illustrate the limitations of professional development that offers a relatively narrow exposure to a topic, with little follow-through and no opportunity to practice with the support of an instructional coach or supervisor. A veteran teacher we know referred to such in-service training as drive-by professional development.

After numerous studies reveal the ineffectiveness of superficial staff development programs (Joyner, 2000), why will the majority of teachers for the coming school year continue to experience the kind of staff development programs represented by the Wood Knoll example? First, Wood Knoll's staff development initiative is *inexpensive.* Except for the honorarium for the day's presenter and the investment in donuts and coffee, there is no other allocation of district resources for consultants, materials, release time, teacher assignments, or changes in schedules. Second, school administrators believe that teachers are *already educated—* as in "She's certified in mathematics." Wood Knoll's staff development program is not intended to *educate* teachers, but to *train* teachers to execute a technique or routine. Third, one-day workshops are typically required by state law—no days need to be added to the school calendar and no teachers need to be released from classes. Fourth, the planning and implementation of the obligatory yet cursory staff development fits well with the managerial role of school administration: ordering food, employing the presenter of the day, copying materials, and constructing a one-day agenda. Fifth, the relentless focus on raising standardized test scores—teaching to a number—generates a "silver-bullet mentality" among teachers and school administrators. Instead of devoting the time, materials, and expertise to develop a comprehensive approach to improving teaching and learning, faculties under the gun to meet Annual Yearly Progress goals look for a relatively simple technique or system.

Finally, drive-by staff development days perpetuate the bargain struck between administrators and teachers: you don't bother me and I won't bother you. The sad truth of school administration is that assuming a leadership role in curriculum and instruction is fraught with all kind of dangers from angry teachers upset with infringements on the sanctity of their classrooms, to community members who believe that schools should teach the way they were taught—the traditional assign-assess model of instruction. Planning a staff development day featuring the technique of the day or complying with the state mandate of the year does not threaten the pedagogical beliefs, organizational structures, and teaching

Figure 5.1   Meeting Agenda

	Wood Knoll School District 582	
	"Where Excellence Is A Tradition"	
	Teacher Workshop Day	
	AGENDA	
	Friday, October 10	
	8:00 a.m.	
	Morgan Auditorium	
8:00—8:30	Coffee and Rolls	Cafeteria
8:30—9:00	Message from the Superintendent *Meeting Performance Goals*	Morgan Auditorium
9:00—9:30	Message from the Principal *Focus on Student Learning*	
9:30—11:30	Dr. Frances Bacon *Data-Driven Teaching*	
11:30—12:30	LUNCH	Cafeteria
12:30—1:30	Learning Communities Breakout Sessions	Team Meeting Rooms
1:30—2:00	Dr. Frances Bacon *What Did We Learn Today?*	Morgan Auditorium
2:00—2:30	Dr. Samuel Johnson, Assistant Superintendent for Curriculum & Instruction *How to Collect and Report Data in Your Classroom* *Data Report Form* *Due Dates*	
2:30—3:00	Content Area Team Meetings *Curriculum Mapping*	Team Meeting Rooms
3:00	Dismissal	

practices that support the "deep structure of schooling" (Tye, 2000, p. 5) in America. Why risk a grievance, faculty morale, or an unpleasant board of education meeting over beliefs and practices of institutional schooling that are firmly entrenched in classrooms and households? It is far safer and far less time-consuming to pursue the *instructional manager* role of scheduler, employer of consultants, distributor of materials, and collector of workshop evaluations.

WHAT WE KNOW ABOUT PROFESSIONAL DEVELOPMENT

The futility of cursory in-service training is verified in decades-long studies of adult learning in professional environments (Hargreaves & Fullan, 1992; Knowles, Swanson, & Holton, 2005; Levine, 1988; Merriam & Caffarella, 1999). Adults will not master ambitious approaches to teaching and learning by sitting in darkened auditoriums, attending conferences, taking a course at a university, or sitting in contrived learning communities (Hargreaves, 1991). In the last decade, the research on effective professional development programs has described general principles of

Principles of Effective Professional Development Programs	
Focus	*Distinctive Features*
Gaps in Performance	Training program is developed to address a discrepancy between desired learning outcomes and actual performance of students on those outcomes.
Teacher Involvement	Teachers identify the discrepancy in performance.
School Based	Training program addresses local performance gaps.
Collaborative	Administrators and teachers design the training program.
Content Rich	Training program stresses the *what* and *why* of a new pedagogy.
Duration	Training program lasts for three to five years.
Resource Rich	Teachers involved in the training program receive the time, materials, space, and expertise necessary to learn a new pedagogy.

adult learning that have demonstrated effective implementation of sophisticated approaches to curriculum and instruction (Blank & de las Alas, 2009; Cohen & Hill, 2000; Desimone, Porter, Garet, Yoon, & Birman, 2002; Garet, Porter, Desimone, Birman, & Yoon, 2001; Hiebert, 1999; Little, 1989, 1993; Wei, Darling-Hammond, Andree, Richardson, & Orphanos, 2009).

THE DISREGARDED TRUTHS OF PROFESSIONAL DEVELOPMENT

The formidable cultural and institutional obstacles that impede the implementation of effective professional development programs should not conceal the truths that we now know about the power of enhancing the knowledge and skills of classroom teachers. We know from the research that *curriculum matters* (Chinn & Malhotra, 2002; Hill et al., 2008; Linn & Muilenburg, 1996; Pintrich, Marx, & Boyle, 1993; Riordan & Noyce, 2001; Saxe, Gearhart, & Nasir, 2001). Educators must have access to configurations of subject matter, materials, and activities that compel students to develop rich understandings of what makers and users of different subject matters do. In all other subject matters, state standards call upon school leaders and teachers to implement curricula that move students from recalling facts and procedures on the customary weekly test to applying that knowledge to messy real-world problems.

We know from the research that *teaching matters* (Darling-Hammond & Bransford, 2005). We can make broad distinctions between two categories of teachers: those teachers who attend to student thinking and design lessons that require their students to employ disciplined ways of thinking about problems; and those teachers who busy themselves with managing routines, organizing activities, and testing information represented in textbooks. Teachers who are unsure of what and how they know a subject either stay one chapter ahead of the students or, even worse, seriously misrepresent subject matter concepts and procedures (Cohen, 1990; Hill et al., 2008).

We know from the research that *organization matters* (Coburn, 2001, 2005; Cohen & Spillane, 1992; Langer, 2001; Stein & Nelson, 2003). In schools where drive-by staff development workshops are the norm, there is little hope that ambitious approaches to curricula will be implemented with integrity. A different picture emerges when administrators understand ambitious approaches to teaching subject matter, when teachers have time to make collective sense out of a new pedagogy, and when experts are readily available to guide innovative approaches to teaching a

---

Fundamental Truths of Schooling

- Curriculum matters
- Teaching matters
- Training matters
- Organization matters

---

new pedagogy. In schools designed as *professional learning cultures*, teachers walk into classrooms knowing that administrators will provide the time, materials, expertise, and most importantly, the trust, to work with ambitious approaches to teaching and learning.

We know from the research that *training matters* (Borko, 2004; Coburn & Russell, 2008; Cohen & Hill, 2000; Stein & Coburn, 2008). Teachers leaving darkened auditoriums after a two-hour presentation have very different understandings of new content standards than teachers invited to participate in extended learning experiences that are content focused, provide opportunities for active learning, and connect with actual classroom experiences.

Given all we know about what good teaching is and the kinds of organizations that deepen teachers' knowledge of good teaching, the question remains: Why do the truths of professional development remain disregarded? The usual response of school administrators is that there is no money and no time. The usual outcome of this response is Wood Knoll's opening day agenda. While access to money, materials, expertise, and time certainly does matter in schools, the failure of professional development programs originates in schools that are *not* designed for learning. The principles of effective professional development programs have been largely ignored by school leaders and teachers who work in schools that are constrained by structures antithetical to reflective practice. Teachers are embedded in classrooms without a coherent understanding of how children learn and of a profession that has become detached from purposeful methods of studying instructional problems.

Two Architectures of Learning

Institutional Learning. School administrators like to say that the schools they lead are "learning organizations." Schools as they are currently situated are not learning organizations—they are institutions. Institutional schooling in America is designed to assign roles, distribute materials, implement programs, and document outcomes. The beliefs, ideas, and practices that guide institutional schooling are grounded in a system of instruction that values certainty, efficiency, and accountability. Institutional models of schooling employ certified teachers (highly qualified), distribute curriculum in boxes, mandate scripted instruction, and rely on forced choice tests to assess student learning. We believe, however, this picture can change.

Professional development in schools designed for production treat gaps in outcomes as a management problem, not a learning problem. School administrators in an institution become instructional *managers,* not instructional *leaders.* When a documented outcome—a test score— falls below the state-mandated score, instructional managers respond by adding to or subtracting from one or more components of institutional schooling. They employ another specialist in this program, enforce the use of *I can* statements, order more technology, or adopt the technique of the day. The learning principle that governs institutional schooling is *imitation*—just adopt a program and implement the technique of the day. Drive-by staff development programs fit well into an organizational model focused on the efficient management of inputs and outputs. Institutional learning completely disregards the truths of effective professional development programs.

Professional Learning. Professional learning environments are designed to embrace the truths of staff development. Instead of a linear process that disregards these truths in favor of the efficient management of inputs and outputs, professional cultures provide the organizational capacity to inquire about an instructional problem or improve the quality of teaching. The outcome of this deliberative process is a training regime that provides teachers with the time, materials, expertise, and forums to develop private understandings and public demonstrations of a new pedagogy or resolution to an instructional problem (Cohen, Raudenbush, & Ball, 2003).

Figure 5.2 represents the components of an instructional system designed to generate ongoing conversations over agreed-upon patterns of instruction that grow students intellectually, emotionally, and socially. In action, the learning process depicted in Figure 5.2 does not represent an isolated staff development program, but a continual process of distributing learning across departments, grade-level teams, or groups of teachers wrestling with the enactment of good teaching and good curriculum. In a professional learning culture, there are persistent references to an agreed-upon pattern of teaching: what is good teaching and what is good curriculum. Departures from an agreed-upon pattern of teaching—what students are experiencing in classrooms—are viewed by administrators and teachers as an instructional problem. The solution to an instructional problem requires the organizational capacity to support purposeful approaches to defining (method of inquiry) and resolving the instructional

Figure 5.2   Professional Learning Response to Gaps in Outcomes

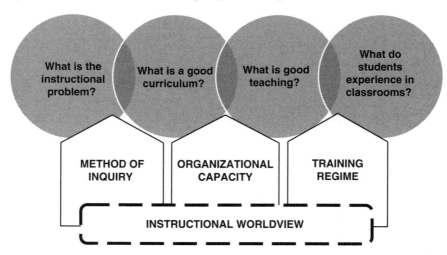

problem (training regime). The glue that bonds the professional learning process together is an instructional worldview that provides administrators and teachers with a vision of why they became educators.

THE COMPONENTS OF A PROFESSIONAL LEARNING CULTURE

Instructional Worldview

Professional development programs only work when they make collective sense (Coburn, 2001, 2005) to administrators and teachers. How does this theory, idea, or practice fit into our philosophy of teaching and learning? Without a clear response to this question, a new technique or theory of learning has nothing to bond with—it merely floats through classrooms, unattached to prior understandings, experiences, or values. Before administrators can contemplate a professional development program, they must work with faculty to develop and articulate what we call an *instructional worldview*. An instructional worldview is a coherent response to questions that philosophers and psychologists have posed about education for centuries. Figure 5.3 portrays each of these fundamental questions of schooling and how they interact with each other to formulate a coherent response to the question: *How do children learn?*

Developing an instructional worldview is not just an intellectual exercise for schools of education. Instructional worldviews guide teachers as they organize and implement academic tasks in their classrooms and predict how students will respond to agreed-upon definitions of

Figure 5.3   The Fundamental Questions of Schooling

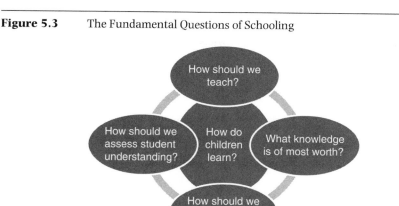

good teaching and good curricula. Table 5.1 illustrates a *Tale of Two Classrooms:* students sitting in *Instructional Worldview I* classrooms will experience significantly different instructional patterns than students sitting in *Instructional Worldview II* classrooms. Students graduating from *Instructional Worldview I* classrooms will think about and represent the subjects they are taught much differently than students enrolled in *Instructional Worldview II.*

Without a coherent response to the fundamental questions of schooling—what is a good curriculum and what is good teaching—administrators and teachers become victims of what we might call the technique of the day—the false separation of the *how* of teaching from the *why* of teaching. Without a coherent understanding of the *why* of a good curriculum and the *why* of good teaching, school administrators and teachers understandably look to "generic" methods that will address some immediate problem in their classrooms ("classroom management") or that are "peripheral" to accurately representing a subject ("using math manipulatives") (Cohen & Hill, 2000, p. 312). The utility of make-and-take workshops, the emotional uplift that comes with listening to an inspirational speaker, and the absence of all that theory-talk are potent forces. They detach school administrators and teachers from the theoretical and general principles that govern the explanatory discourses of their profession and the glue that keeps instructional initiative attached to the classroom wall.

Method of Inquiry

Embedded in professional learning environments is an agreed-upon *method of inquiry* that imposes order on the myriad of theories, behaviors,

Table 5.1   Tale of Two Classrooms

Classroom Element	Instructional Worldview I	Instructional Worldview II
Goals	• Interpreting, evaluating, reasoning • Relational, imaginative	• Rules, routines, procedures • Logical
Discourse	• Discussion • Divergent questions	• Lecture • Convergent questions
Materials	• Teachers modify commercial products and/or author their own materials • Primary works	• Textbook • Commercial worksheets, games, tests
Activities	• Small groups • Role playing • Debate • Panels • Student presentations • Labs	• Seatwork/silent reading • Teacher directed questions • Drill • Completion of worksheets • Media presentations (DVD, PowerPoint)
Organization of Knowledge	• Themes • Concepts • Big ideas/big questions	• Units • Chapters • Objectives
Outcomes	• Authentic product • Performance	• Passing a test • Completing commercially prepared materials

emotions, activities, and information that fly around classrooms. Since instructional problems are situated in particular classrooms in particular communities, there is no one method of inquiry. An agreed-upon method of inquiry does not need to meet the rigors of academic research studies. What is mandatory, however, is that all professional development programs begin with a process that defines a problem; seeks out theories, ideas, and practices that govern the identified problem; develops a plan of action that includes a home-grown formulation of a theory-driven instructional approach; and articulates the consequences of an agreed-upon plan of action.

It is understandable that the difficulty of managing the uncertainties of classrooms tempts administrators and teachers to look for quick answers—the technique of the day—rather than to spend time participating in a deliberate process of asking questions, interpreting research, and predicting consequences. Adhering to an agreed-upon *method of inquiry*, however, is the foundation of reflective practice. Administrators and teachers cannot develop an understanding of an instructional

---

A Method of Inquiry

- What is the problem?
- How do we know it is a problem?
- What theories, ideas, and practices govern this problem?
- How might we solve this problem?
- What plan of action should we pursue to address the problem?
- What would be the consequences of our plan of action?
- What criteria would we use to determine if we have solved the problem?

Functions of Inquiry

- Requires administrators and teachers to confront self-justifying explanations for the discrepancy between accepted teaching repertoires and what the research says is good teaching
- Establishes a norm for looking at teaching practices objectively and critically
- Presents a process for substantiating what we know to be true and what we know to be false about an instructional problem
- Avoids personal criticisms of individuals who promote different instructional perspectives
- Documents the history of an instructional problem
- Sets up a quiet space between action and contemplation

---

strategy—where you are, where you want to go, and when you arrive—without a disciplined way of thinking about an instructional problem—a method of inquiry. If done well, the functions of inquiry make transparent the beliefs, intentions, opinions, and practices that remain hidden behind classroom doors. No professional development program can succeed until there is an honest conversation about what teachers believe to be true and what we can prove to be true. We understand that teachers' beliefs direct their actions, and we understand further that humans are most likely to fixate beliefs based on what they discover, especially through an inquiry process, rather than based on what they are told to believe.

Organizational Capacity

No matter how well administrators design and orchestrate the components of a professional learning environment, the willingness of teachers to actively engage in the difficult process of exchanging core

---

Where Questions

- **Where** will we get the time?
- **Where** will we get the materials?
- **Where** will we get the expertise?
- **Where** will we get the space?
- **Where** will we get the training?
- **Where** will we get the money?

---

teaching practices for unfamiliar theory-driven pedagogies is contingent on the kinds of answers administrators give to, what we term, *where questions.*

Some administrators view these questions as attempts by teachers to avoid work or to oppose new approaches to curriculum. *Where* questions are genuine responses to theories, ideas, and practices that challenge teachers and may require a radical change in a teaching identity. Edicts cannot change patterns of behavior constructed from years of education, training, and practice. In the best designed professional development programs, teachers' instructional identities are gradually changed over a period of time in environments they determine to be friendly to their efforts to experiment with new theories, ideas, and practices of instruction. The essential condition for transforming deeply held and valued teaching practices is trusting that the schools they work in will give teachers the time, the space, the materials, the expertise, and the forums to make collective sense out of new approaches to teaching and learning.

Training Regimes

The most obvious, and yet most ignored, component of professional learning environments, is *training.* While the private sector invests heavily on continually improving the knowledge and skills of their employees, schools pay little attention to the process of acquiring the knowledge and skills to properly enact sophisticated approaches to curriculum and instruction. It is not unusual in schools to implement inquiry-based approaches to teaching math and science, a whole language reading program, or a thematic social studies program with little more than a one- or two-day workshop. At times, schools implement new initiatives with even less—only a perfunctory opening day comment by the principal—"The new reading program will be delivered to your classrooms this afternoon."

Administrators normally blame a lack of money for poorly designed professional development programs. Certainly organizational capacity

Table 5.2   Fundamental Principles of Adult (and Student) Learning

Principle of Learning	*Application*
Learning must be active, not passive.	Teachers must be situated in a process that develops a personal understanding of how a theory looks and works in the classroom.
Learning must be content-based.	Teachers must be situated in a process that develops an understanding of the theory as well as the practice of a new pedagogy.
Learning must be risk free.	Teachers must be situated in a process where they feel free to experiment (and make mistakes).
Learning must respect teaching identities.	Teachers must be situated in a process that respects their prior beliefs about teaching and learning—their teaching identity.
Learning must pay attention to where a teacher comes from.	Teachers must be situated in a process that establishes connections between what they practice in classrooms and the theories, ideas, and methods of a new pedagogy.
Learning is interpretative.	Teachers must be situated in a process that is comfortable with differing expressions of a new pedagogy.
Practice makes perfect.	Teachers must be situated in a process that provides an **extended** process of unlearning → relearning → interpreting → practice.
Learning is socially constructed.	Teachers must be situated in a process that promotes extended conversations over the meaning and application of a new pedagogy.

plays an important role in a training regime. But money is not the reason schools do teacher training so badly. In fact, the mistake most school administrators make is talking about cost and schedules first. Their design for teacher learning amounts to creating an agenda for the day. School administrators assume that if they do a good job at gathering resources for a professional development initiative, the training will take care of itself. Even if a training strategy emerges out of a staff development planning session, the program will be built around the organizational requirements of institutional schooling rather than how adults (and students) acquire and practice sophisticated theories, principles, and concepts in curriculum and instruction (see Table 5.2). A well designed training regime focuses not on organizational needs, but on negotiating the divide between the practical wisdom of classroom teaching and formal knowledge of curriculum and instruction.

The Process of Adult Learning

To apply these principles of adult learning, school leaders must treat professional development as a process—not an event. Figure 5.4 represents the learning process administrators and teachers must undergo to master new understandings and methods in curriculum and instruction. Table 5.3 summarizes the tasks in that learning process. Those who make the decision to engage in a purposeful approach to learning a new pedagogy must embed themselves in a learning process that adheres to stages and functions of the training regime pictured in Figure 5.4 (*A–H*). Administrators and teachers grappling with the meaning and application of a new instructional initiative will have different experiences with the progression of tasks in the training regime. The real world of messy classrooms, uncertainties of theory-driven pedagogies, and the particular social context of their school are all variables that affect their experience. It is critical to hold on to a process where *all* of the principles of adult learning interact with each other in a way that results in administrators and teachers *owning* an interpretation of a new instructional initiative.

Figure 5.4   Stages of the Training Regime

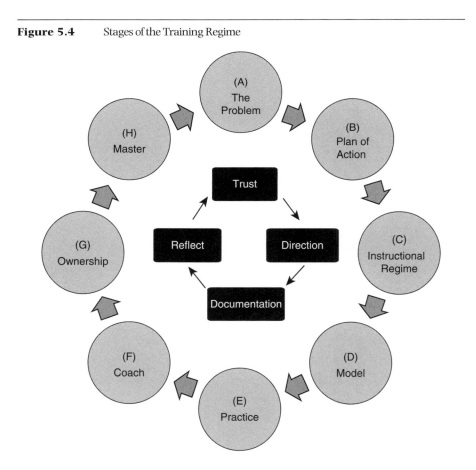

The training regime summarized in Figure 5.4 and Table 5.3 is a different cultural model of learning than most teachers experience in American schools. Most staff development programs in our country are designed for institutional learning: They begin with Stage *A* (the problem) and end with a Stage *B* (a plan of action)—amounting to presentations in darkened auditoriums or boxes delivered to classrooms. Teachers subjected to institutional learning are asked (or directed in some cases) to replicate new instructional theories and practices that are presented in manuals, from stages, or in one-day workshops. Administrators directing institutional learning are asked to distribute

Table 5.3   Tasks of a Training Regime

	Component	*What Teachers Are Asked to Do*
A	**Problem**	Identify gaps between a valued end of schooling and actual student performance
B	**Plan of Action**	Develop a purposeful plan of action (problem → theory → hypothesis → organizational capacity → training regime) to resolve an instructional problem or gap in performance
C	**Instructional Regime**	Follow a general pattern of arranging and presenting instructional materials, activities, and subject matter to adopt curricula, design professional development programs, supervise teacher performance, and employ faculty
D	**Model**	Observe expert performance of agreed-upon patterns of applying materials, activities, subject matter, and classroom discourse
E	**Practice**	Under the supervision of a mentor/consultant, enact in classrooms the agreed-upon patterns of applying materials, activities, subject matter, and classroom discourse
F	**Coach**	Participate in ongoing conversations with mentor/consultant on gaps between the intentions of theory-based methods and actual implementation of those methods in classrooms
G	**Ownership**	Construct pedagogical approaches and a plan of action that agree with a school's instructional worldview, the social context of the school, and preexisting experiences of teachers
H	**Master**	Present → model → coach → practice an agreed-upon instructional pattern until it becomes a regular component of a teaching repertoire

the right materials, hire the right consultant, and hold teachers accountable for implementing the theory or practice of the day. For teachers, institutional learning results in surface representations of an instructional theory or method. For administrators, institutional learning results in walking around with clipboards checking off the surface representations of new instructional methodologies. Institutional learning cares little about understanding or ownership; it cares a lot about completing checklists.

BUILDING BLOCKS OF PROFESSIONAL LEARNING

While the stages and functions of the training regime are necessary for mastering new approaches to curriculum and instruction, they are not sufficient for providing direction for defining the training regime or for developing a culture of continuous learning. At the core of effective training regimes are administrators who take responsibility for providing the organizational capacity to direct and orchestrate the stages and tasks of a training regime. In order to perform the delicate job of bringing a group of teachers together to resolve an instructional problem, administrators must skillfully choreograph the *building blocks of professional learning.*

Trust

The essential building block of professional learning is an environment of trust in teacher workspaces. Administrators fashion an environment of trust around three behaviors. First, significant discourse within teacher workspaces is fixed on descriptions and explanations for what constitutes high-quality teaching and what is being observed in classrooms. In Chapter 3, we suggest a process for initiating the instructional conversations that focus on defining high-quality teaching. The outcome of these instructional conversations is a plan for modifying the training regime in order to move closer to an agreed-upon performance of new pedagogy. Second, all participants involved in a training regime are expected to respectfully listen to each other. Respectful listening requires fully listening to participants' contributions, setting aside judgments, asking questions for clarification, and openly ruminating about connections between theoretical understandings of pedagogy and personal understandings of that pedagogy in action. Third, administrators build trust in a training regime when they provide teachers with the time, materials, space, expertise, and organizational configurations to fully master new approaches to curriculum and instruction.

Direction

Teachers lose interest in training regimes when they become stuck in one or more stages of the regime or become disconnected from a valued end of schooling. It is reasonable for a teacher to ask, "Why are we learning this new instructional strategy?" School leadership must assume the responsibility for moving teachers in and out of each stage of the training regime. To retain trust within the training regime, moving teachers in and out of each stage is a consensual agreement reached among consultants, mentors, supervisors, and the teachers involved. As we note in greater detail in Chapter 4, whatever stage teachers find themselves in, school leaders must provide them with the resources and expert mentoring to help them accomplish the difficult tasks of questioning what works for them in the classroom and mastering unfamiliar instructional strategies. Again, the idea is not simply to influence teachers to mimic set routines, but to follow the heuristic procedures that distinguish exceptional teachers and that feature a manageable set of considerations that have a great impact on learning and achievement.

More important than resources and proper assistance is the establishment of a training goal that is more expansive than simply learning a theory, idea, or new teaching routine. Teachers can become quickly disenchanted with a training regime whose goals are narrowly focused on an institutional outcome—raise a test score, imitate a technique of the day, or document compliance with accountability mandates. Teachers are more likely to persist in a training regime designed around the goals of raising the level of student discourse, developing deep understandings of subject matter, or moving student thinking from mere recall of information to the ability to reason well.

Documentation

Training regimes designed for making collective sense of a theory-driven instructional strategy value a process where teachers are positioned in forums where they can talk a lot about the application of instructional theories, concepts, and ideas. The process of collective sense-making produces a lot of terminology, concepts, frameworks, stories, metaphors, and artifacts that participants believe faithfully represent the enactment of a new instructional strategy. School leaders must assume the responsibility for making public (documenting) the material representations of the abstractions of theory-talk. Documenting what teachers are saying, doing, and constructing provides all participants in the training regime with a navigational tool for moving the training regime in the right direction. To properly document, teachers require a venue where they are able to discuss the instructional meaning of artifacts produced during the training regime—lesson plans, worksheets, lesson presentations, activity structures, and conceptual frameworks. These public viewing sessions provide the space, time, and access to expertise to understand the relationship between the abstractions of theory-talk and tangible products of teacher practice.

Reflection

Thinking and talking about what we know, what we are doing, what we *should* know and what we *should* be doing in the classrooms is an activity in the training regime that keeps professional learning cultures honest. Since it is difficult to change comfortable teaching repertoires, a training regime might result in an interpretation of a theory-driven instructional strategy that may work in the classroom, but may not represent the substance and form of the instructional theory, concept, or practice. To maintain the integrity of a newly adopted instructional practice, school leaders must be persistent in probing teachers to talk about their understandings of the substance and form of a theory-driven instructional strategy. The nature and tone of reflective questioning is not accusatory, and a supervisor does not need to be the one to facilitate reflective conversations. Instructional coaches, mentors, and other colleagues can engage with teachers to help them to plan and evaluate the effect of instructional decisions. The goal of reflective questioning is always focused on asking teachers to articulate what they are doing in classrooms and how these instructional moves faithfully represent an agreed-upon approach to teaching knowledge or skills. The underlying motive of this goal is moving teachers from talking about their intentions and frustrations to analyzing what actually occurred in their classrooms. Reflective conversations are always anchored in a purposeful approach to asking teachers why they did what they did, how what they did relates to theory-driven instructional initiative, and what were the documented instructional outcomes of the lesson. We discuss these kind of reflective interchanges in greater detail in Chapter 6.

Analyzing and acting upon the discrepancy between what teachers say they are doing in classrooms and what students actually end up doing becomes the engine that drives an instructional system focused on what matters most in schools—teaching. Throughout this book, we are describing how components of this system—induction, mentoring, professional development, and teacher evaluation—are woven together by instructional leaders to form a culture dedicated to growing teachers' knowledge and practice. At the center of professional growth cultures

---

Reflective Questioning

As you think about your understandings of the new instructional strategy, consider these questions:

- How are students responding to the new strategy?
- What evidence do we have that students are responding in ways that represent the goals of the agreed-upon strategy?
- How do your work products represent the substance and form of the new strategy?
- What frustrations are you experiencing with the new strategy?
- How might I assist you in realizing the goals of the new strategy?

---

are venues that promote the habits of what Dewey (1938) would call intelligent action:

- willingness to study new theories of instruction
- willingness to experiment with new pedagogies
- willingness to challenge weak reasoning
- willingness to open oneself to critiques by colleagues

LEADING PROFESSIONAL LEARNING COMMUNITIES

By now it should be apparent that leadership matters in developing professional learning communities. This chapter provides school administrators with a guide for developing professional development programs that honor adult learning principles (see Table 5.2) and provide teachers with a process for developing a new instructional identity. While this chapter provides administrators with a blueprint for designing a culture of continuous learning, it does not elaborate on the knowledge and skills an administrator must acquire to build a professional learning culture. School administrators who decide to become architects of professional learning cultures must become expert at the *functions of collective sense-making*. We list these functions in Table 5.4.

SUMMARY

Chapter 5 describes the substance and form of two cultural models of professional development that administrators and teachers participate

Table 5.4   Functions of Collective Sense-Making

Purposing	The self-discipline required to change an instructional identity requires an end in view that teachers personally value. Teachers entered the profession to educate young people, not raise test scores. Architects of professional learning cultures have the ability to articulate a vision of what it means to be educated.
Framing	The continuous improvement of good teaching requires a coherent response to the fundamental questions of schooling (see Figure 5.3). Architects of professional learning cultures have the knowledge to discern the instructional theories, ideas, and practices that would grow a school's instructional worldview and those that would not.
Knowing	Purposing an instructional program and properly framing an instructional problem require an understanding of the theories, ideas, and practices that are introduced into classrooms and teacher workspaces. Architects of professional learning cultures engage in a private journey of acquiring an understanding of the theories, ideas, and practices that grow their schools' instructional worldview.
Conversing	New instructional identities are developed over time in social situations where teachers are able to talk to colleagues, mentors, consultants, and administrators about their personal understandings and applications of a new instructional strategy. Architects of professional learning cultures possess the content knowledge and interpersonal skills to initiate and sustain conversations that allow teachers to make connections between theory-talk and practice-talk.
Organizing	The willingness of teachers to stay the course in a training regime depends solely on the response to *where* questions. Architects of professional learning cultures possess the management skills to gather, allocate, and systematize the resources teachers require to understand and practice new instructional strategies.

in each year. School administrators who are asked to implement institutional learning programs become expert at assigning responsibility, distributing materials, hiring presenters, and walking through classrooms with clipboards filled with lists of components of a new instructional strategy. Teachers subjected to institutional learning know that programs presented at the opening institute day will disappear over time. Teachers in schools with professional learning cultures are provided the time, space, materials, and expertise to develop personal understandings of the theory and practice of a new instructional strategy. The process of unlearning comfortable teaching repertoires and relearning theories, ideas, and practices that enhance a school's instructional worldview requires a training regime that is properly resourced and embraces the principles of adult learning. While components of a professional learning culture are necessary for learning sophisticated instructional strategies, they are not sufficient. Ultimately, the realization of a school's instructional worldview in classrooms is wholly dependent on the ability of school leaders to skill-fully perform the functions of collective sense-making.

QUESTIONS FOR DISCUSSION AND REFLECTION

1. Think about the teaching that goes on in your building and describe your school's predominant instructional worldview. In your view, what parts of your school's instructional worldview are working well and what parts are not working so well?

2. Teachers often complain about staff development programs that have too much theory-talk and not enough practice-talk. In your view, what role should theory or research play in learning a new instructional strategy? Think about an instructional strategy that has worked for you and describe the role, if any, that theory played in learning and implementing that instructional strategy.

3. When you think about an instructional problem in your building, what processes do administrators and teachers employ to resolve the problem? How does this process compare with the *method of inquiry* described in this chapter?

4. How do administrators in your school build trust among faculty? In your view, what behaviors and policies build trust and what behaviors and policies create distrust? If you were asked to design a professional development program that required teachers to significantly change core teaching practices, how would you build trust into the learning experience?

5. In designing a professional development program, how could you guarantee an unrelenting focus on high-quality instruction? How would you assure that the focus extends over multiple school years?

ACTION STEPS FOR PROFESSIONAL DEVELOPMENT

→ Consult with a team of school leaders to identify the focus for a cohesive professional development plan.

→ Devise a one-year and three-year plan for professional development that will honor principles of adult learning and will promote key instructional practices.

→ Work with a team of school leaders to plan the details of professional experiences that require an inquiry-based approach and provide for follow-through support for teachers.

Summary of Action Steps

How can teacher evaluation become more meaningful?   **6**

The previous chapters describe several crucial administrative activities that should align with a community-specific concept of quality teaching. Another key activity is the evaluation of the teaching staff. Most commonly, this duty is a deficit model that emphasizes the finding of deficiencies and the offering of prescriptions to correct the deficiencies. We judge that a professional growth model for teacher evaluation that values the teacher as an agent in his or her own professional growth offers the most promise to maintain the kind of instructional conversations that have some hope of advancing the quality of teaching.

We see the following imagined scene as representative of the kind of conversation that follows too often from a formal classroom observation, and we confess to having participated in such episodes. We judge that such opportunities for coaching and reflection are critical, and the lost opportunity is almost tragic. We reflect below on the implications associated with this interchange, and later we offer a contrasting model that emphasizes the mutual effort toward professional growth.

"DRIVE-BY" TEACHER EVALUATION

Jones's (1985) study of teacher evaluation policies and procedures revealed teacher evaluation systems in the same condition as the drive-by staff development systems described in Chapter 5, and still common today. The Jones study reports that it was rare that a teacher would be observed twice a year. Even if an administrator stopped in the room, the observation was brief—"I have to get into the halls"—and congratulatory—"you're doing a great job." The vignette beginning on page 108 reveals what such "drive-by" experiences look like.

107

Bob, thanks so much for coming down on such short notice. I've fallen behind in my evaluation schedule. I have to get thirty-five teachers done by the March board meeting. That new football field is taking up more time than I thought. Do you have any questions about the write-up?

Yes, just a couple, Dr. Peters.

Bob, just a minute. I forgot to tell Jane to change the bell schedule—we have that pep assembly this afternoon. (Dr. Peters excuses himself for a brief consultation with his secretary.)

Sorry, Bob, where were we?

Dr. Peters, I have some questions about my write-up.

Go ahead, Bob. We have some time. Let me see. Yes, this period ends at 9:45, right. That's about twenty-five minutes. Wait. Let me get your write-up. Here it is, right where Jane left it last night.

Any problems, Bob?

I don't understand some of the ratings on my observation report.

Tell you the truth, Bob, we are all having trouble with this new evaluation rubric. There's a lot of terminology that hasn't been defined well. Making distinctions between "proficient" and "distinguished" is really something all of us on the administrative team are struggling with. I think in a year or two we will get it straightened out. I think all of us on the administrative team feel that until we get these ratings straightened out that we give the benefit of the doubt to the teacher. You should also know that the administrative team decided that in our first year of using the new instrument no teacher should receive a "distinguished" rating.

Dr. Peters, that was one of my questions. In past years, I have been commended for my knowledge of subject matter. Earning that master's degree several years ago really gave me the knowledge I needed to organize subject matter in a more meaningful way for students.

Bob, no one questions your knowledge of subject matter. You do a great job with getting students ready for Scholastic Bowl. But we felt administratively that no teacher in the building is at the "distinguished" level yet. In another year or two, teachers would work themselves up to that level.

Well, Dr. Peters, in this category 1a, what do I have to do to move from "solid knowledge," to "extensive knowledge"?

Bob, just do what you have been doing. I can guarantee you that when you are up for evaluation in two years you will be at the "distinguished" level. Is it 9:30 already? Time flies on assembly days. Any other questions, Bob?

What about element "2b, Establishing a Culture for Learning?" I think everyone in the building would agree that I generate a lot of "passion" and "student energy" in my history course. Evaluators have noted the high energy levels in my room.

Bob, again, there is no question that you run a high-energy history program. But we are still feeling this new evaluation plan out. The consultant who helped us design this plan really cautioned us against giving anyone a "distinguished" rating the first year. As I said before, don't worry about it. In two years, you will do OK in this area.

(Continued)

Is that the bell ringing? I have to get out in the halls, Bob. Have you signed the document?

Yes, I signed it, but I would still like to talk to you about some of the "basic" ratings.

Bob, I gave out basic ratings in all areas where I didn't observe the behavior in the classroom.

Those basic ratings bother me. Could you come into some more classes to observe those behaviors? It's impossible to observe all these behaviors in an observation that lasted twenty minutes.

Bob, I'm really sorry about having to leave your class early that day. The superintendent is really on us about attending those strategic planning sessions. Don't worry about those "basic" ratings. All of us on the administrative team agreed to rate "basic" for any behavior we did not see. Really, when you think about it, even with more visits, how are you going to observe all sixty-six behaviors? Anyway, Bob, I have to run. Could you give the report to Jane when you leave? Maybe before the end of the year, I'm going to try to get into some more of your classes. See you tonight at the bonfire.

Since that review of teacher evaluation plans, accountability-minded state legislatures have required school districts to develop evaluation plans that specify effective teaching behaviors and procedures for how those behaviors should be assessed. It is clear from reading these accountability mandates that state lawmakers believe that the main role of school administration is supervising teachers. Some accountability mandates have gone further by stipulating the amount of time school administrators should be spending in the role of instructional leader.

The volume and urgent tone of these accountability mandates, however, has not significantly changed the practice of drive-by teacher evaluations. A more recent study of the status of teacher evaluation in public education (Toch & Rothman, 2008) found that the "single, fleeting classroom visit by the principal" (p. 2) continues to be the sole experience teachers have with instructional supervision. The theme we have pursued in this book is that *teaching matters most*, yet we know that the state of teacher supervision in our country amounts to little more than teaching matters least. The question remains: How can this "potentially powerful level of teacher and school improvement" (Toch & Rothman, 2008, p. 1) be transformed into a meaningful process for improving the quality of teacher instruction?

"ABSENTEE LANDLORDS"

In the middle of a flood of rules and regulations mandating the intensification of classroom supervision, school administrators continue to assume the role of "absentee landlords" (Sarason, 2004). A quick look at administrators' calendars for a week will find most of their time allotted to management functions and very little time devoted to the supervisory functions. In truth, as in the case of Bob's experience with teacher evaluation in the previous vignette, the supervision function only shows up on administrative calendars in the month of February. Scheduling preconferences, observations, and postconferences in one-hour intervals provides school supervisors with just the right amount of time to complete all evaluations in time for staffing decisions made at the March board of education meeting. Of course, keeping up this frantic pace for one month out of the year leads to sloppy supervision. Preconferences become notices of time and date of an observation, observations become walk-throughs, postconferences become signing ceremonies, and employment decisions become acclamations. And as February comes to an end, there are a lot of loose ends. Nancy is still struggling with discipline and Fred is becoming negative about kids. Chris is teaching her first-year lessons in her tenth year, and then there is Harriet, who represents a complex of problems. Maybe after the March board meeting and when budgets are finished there will be time to work with Nancy, Fred, and Chris—but there won't be enough time to work sufficiently with Harriet.

Administrators will readily admit that they feel their approach to teacher evaluation is often rushed and perfunctory. At the same time, administrators would point to school calendars that leave little time to properly exercise their supervisory functions. Administrators who faithfully enter classrooms to improve instruction receive little or no reward for their efforts. Aside from the social, emotional, and intellectual turmoil that often accompanies the supervisory function, administrators know full well that the evaluation plans they are carrying out are not designed to augment a professional learning culture. The role of supervisors in an institutional learning culture is simple—comply with teacher evaluation procedures and meet district timelines for personnel recommendations. Both goals of institutional evaluation instruments not only create a toxic supervisory environment, but also ignore the moral and intellectual disconnect between evaluation plans designed for institutional outcomes and evaluation plans designed for optimizing professional learning cultures.

Table 6.1 presents a profile of two very different models of teacher evaluation. *Institutional* learning cultures adopt teacher evaluation plans whose sole goal is holding teachers accountable for implementing a set of prescribed teaching behaviors. *Professional* learning cultures adopt teacher evaluation plans whose sole goal is supporting a process for thinking systematically about the practice of teaching. Supervisors in institutional cultures inspect classrooms, document the absence or presence of prescribed teaching behaviors, and assign ratings based on

Table 6.1   Institutional Versus Professional Teacher Evaluation Plans

Content	*Institutional Evaluations (Accountability)*	*Professional Evaluations (Continuous Growth)*
Goals	• Standardize teaching behaviors • Maintain hierarchy	• Optimize teaching identities • Develop trust and rapport
Organizational Functions	• Hiring • Promotion • Tenure • Dismissal	• Professional development • Mentoring • Coaching • Inquiry
Activities	• Monologues • Supervising • Presenting • Monitoring	• Conversations • Coaching • Modeling • Experimentation
Process	• Preconference • Observation • Write-up • Postconference • Summative evaluation	• Listening • Educating • Modeling • Observing • Practicing • Authoring
Professional Outcomes	• Technician • Dependent • Rule bound	• Reflective practitioner • Empowering • Flexible

teacher implementation of prescribed teaching behaviors. Supervisors in professional learning cultures engage teachers in ongoing conversations about curriculum and instruction, assist teachers with making collective sense out of theory-driven instructional initiatives, and provide the time, space, materials, and expertise to construct new instructional identities. Institutional supervision manages a long list of teaching criteria; professional supervision grows the social, emotional, and intellectual constituents of a teacher's identity.

LISTS AND RUBRICS ABOUND

Applied in an institutional learning culture, teacher evaluation documents are designed to hold teachers accountable and to meet administrative deadlines. Figure 6.2 is an example of a performance evaluation instrument perfectly suited for accountability: it accounts for the presence or absence of prescribed teaching behaviors; it documents the presence of supervisors in classrooms; and it provides administrators with an efficient vehicle for drive-by evaluations. Wood Knoll's instrument, however, is

Figure 6.2   Wood Knoll School District 582 (Performance Evaluation)

Teacher: _____   Dates of observation: _____

Evaluator: _____   Rating: (E) Excellent; (U) Unsatisfactory

INDICATORS OF EFFECTIVE TEACHING (1 = Satisfactory; 2 = Unsatisfactory; 3 = Not Observed)	1	2	3
1. Knowledgeable about subject matter			
2. Demonstrates enthusiasm for subject matter			
3. Uses district curriculum materials			
4. Follows district lesson plan format			
5. Motivated students			
6. Uses technology			
7. High level of student engagement			
8. Discipline is fair and equitable			
9. Connects with students			
10. Redirects off-task behavior			
11. Bulletin boards reflected learning theme of the month			
12. Instruction was "bell-to-bell"			
13. State standard for the day posted in classroom			
14. Creates a respectful classroom environment			
15. Begins class with a "bell-ringer"			
16. Ends class with "closure" activity			
17. Grades are assigned fairly and impartially			
18. Uses positive reinforcement			
19. Remains poised			
20. Displays six pillars of character in class			
21. Prepares students to be life-long learners			
22. Reflects values in district mission statement			
23. Follows district attendance and tardy policy			
24. Is a team player			
25. Attends extracurricular activities			
RECOMMENDATIONS			
Teacher Signature:	Date: ____/____/____		
Supervisor Signature:			

poorly suited for growing a teacher's pedagogical skills. Wood Knoll is an imaginary school, but the instrument represents an amalgam of the kinds of instruments we have seen in schools.

Setting aside criteria that have nothing to do with effective teaching (4, 11, 12, 13, 20, 22, 23, 24, and 25), the remaining indicators leave supervisors groping for descriptions and explanations for meaningful relationships between the listed abstractions of theory and teachers' efforts to make sense out of the social, emotional, and intellectual currents flowing around their classrooms. Instead of a professional learning instrument designed to make collective sense of sophisticated approaches to curriculum and instruction, Wood Knoll's instrument positions administrators and teachers in offices trying to unravel the meaning of eclectic lists of "performance indicators"— indicators that are part cherry-picked variables from research studies, part remnants of old teaching models (and past evaluation plans), part district idiosyncratic beliefs about what is effective teaching, and part job responsibilities that district administrators feel teachers should be performing better. Any attempt by a supervisor or teacher to use Wood Knoll's instrument to grow professionally is quickly dissipated in postobservation conferences that become definitional nightmares: "Why did I receive *satisfactory* for number nineteen '*remains poised*' in class?"

What gets lost in definitional games and dog and pony shows, is a meaningful process for mastering an agreed-upon instructional repertoire that aims at the kinds of critical and creative thinking skills so often listed in district mission statements and curriculum guides. Professional learning organizations like the Association for Supervision and Curriculum Development (ASCD) and professional certification bodies like Educational Testing Service (ETS) are attempting to remedy local notions of effective teaching by constructing evaluation instruments that are research based and contain procedures that will grow the professional knowledge of teachers. In their ASCD publication, *Teacher Evaluation: To Enhance Professional Practice*, Charlotte Danielson and Thomas L. McGreal (2000) provide a "blueprint" for achieving the dual purposes of accountability and professional development (p. 10). Danielson and McGreal's framework for enhanced professional practice offers the following recommendations for merging the goals of perceived needs for accountability with goals for growing teachers' pedagogical knowledge:

- establishing different expectations, timelines, and procedures for teachers with varying levels of experience
- gathering multiple sources of information such as classroom observations, self-assessments, and planning documents to determine levels of performance

- taking into account the social context of the classroom (for example, grade level, subject taught, student diversity)
- requiring that all supervisors be adequately trained to make reliable and valid judgments about teacher performance

While these adjustments make the teacher evaluation process more credible to teachers, they also expose an evaluation system in need of refinement. We believe that teacher evaluation, when approached as a collaborative effort to promote professional growth, is an integral component of continually improving the quality of classroom teaching. Decades of tinkering with lists, rubrics, and documentation have had little influence on the quality of teaching and on the quality of students' experience in American schools. The ever-growing number of effective teaching criteria, elaborate rubrics, and formulation of value-added scores continues to assume that good teaching amounts to merely pushing the lists, rubrics, and scores into classrooms. Good teaching does not originate from replicating long lists of teaching criteria in classrooms. Good teaching is always an act of interpreting how best to organize subject matter, materials, and activities based on an assessment of student skills and interests. To fully realize the potential that teacher evaluation could play in focusing administrators and teachers on quality classroom instruction requires that administrators acknowledge the two realities inside teaching. First, teachers are agents. No matter what the state standards say, what models of teaching are prescribed, or what the test scores show, teachers will impart a particular interpretation on how materials, subject matter, activity structures, and assignments are organized for learning. That interpretation must reflect the intellectual, social, and emotional needs of the students being taught. Second, teacher evaluation is a process, not an event. Teacher evaluation plans must move from inspectorial goals to professional growth goals.

Establishing a norm of teacher agency and continuous learning in teacher evaluation instruments should rest on three essential beliefs. First, teachers will not experiment with sophisticated approaches to teaching subject matter in school environments that are fear-injected. In *practice*, this means that talk of ratings and performance levels must be minimized or muted in the professional growth model. Second, making collective sense out of new instructional strategies is a highly social process involving administrators and teachers in extended conversations over what they understand, what they observe, what they practice. Eventually these instructional conversations author a definition of effective teaching. In practice, professional growth models continually clarify the relationship among these factors: what learning outcomes a teacher intends to accomplish; how those intentions are represented in subject matter; how teachers organize activity structures to achieve the purpose and accurate representation of subject matter; and how the lesson design draws a student into pursuing an understanding of a topic. Third, students will experience good teaching in all classrooms when faculties are guided by a common understanding of what constitutes quality instruction. In practice, all decisions related to curriculum, instruction, assessment, and learning environment agree with a school's instructional worldview.

Professional growth models would clearly be opposed to another list of effective teaching criteria and inspectorial processes for checking on teacher implementation of one criterion indicator after another. Professional growth models do advance a process for assisting teachers with authoring public and private understandings of ambitious approaches to teaching and learning. The teacher evaluation process that emerges from this process requires that administrators and teachers enter into a deliberative process over the question—How do I improve on good teaching? If staged correctly, the act of evaluating teacher performance moves from a game of trying to guess what is on the evaluator's mind to a method of inquiry into how teachers can personalize a school's definition of good teaching. Rather than prompting reflection on an administrator's agenda or institutional definitions of effective teaching, professional growth models immerse teachers in a continual process of thinking about, talking about, and acting upon gaps that exist between a school's definition of good teaching and how that definition is applied in particular classrooms. The improvement of good teaching demands that the teacher evaluation process joins definitions of good teaching with a process that is composed of the following features.

Collaboration

Teachers participating in the professional growth process will become a member of an evaluation team that comes together to observe, discuss, model, and practice gaps between agreed-upon definitions of good teaching and actual classroom performance. The composition of the team should contain enough members (three to five) to provide multiple perspectives on lesson design and implementation. Each member of the team should possess the subject matter background and grade-level experience to intelligently participate in an examination of the implementation of particular content knowledge and skills. One member of the team should be schooled in current understandings of the theories, ideas, concepts, and practices governing the instructional strategies that are being practiced for a particular instructional context.

Essential Acts of Good Teaching

Teachers participating in the professional growth process will focus on the essential elements of a lesson: purpose, representation of subject matter, activity structures, nature of teacher/student relationships, and student products.

Inquiry

Teachers participating in the professional growth process will work with peers on resolving problems and gaps they have identified in implementing a school's definition of good teaching. The process will recognize teachers' roles as action researchers and employ a purposeful process of resolving an instructional problem:

- What is the problem?
- How do we know it is a problem?
- What do we know about the problem?
- What are some options for solving the problem?
- What will I need to know and practice to solve the problem?
- Who will contribute with me in studying the data and discussing their implications and significance?
- How do we know when we have solved the problem?
- How will we share what we have learned so that others benefit?

Documentation

Teachers participating in the professional growth process will produce artifacts like lesson plans, videos, assessments, activity structures, or conceptual frameworks that demonstrate mastery of an essential act of teaching or the resolution of an instructional problem. The products of the professional growth process will be archived in areas that are readily accessible to all teachers.

Performances

Teachers participating in the professional growth process will be asked to present in appropriate venues the methods and outcomes they employed or produced to master an essential act of teaching or solve an instructional problem.

Professional Development

Teachers participating in the professional growth process will be expected to contribute to the planning and implementation of training regimes relating to the mastery of an essential act of teaching or a shared instructional problem.

New Professional Growth Framework

School districts that embrace the norm of professional growth discard the beliefs, content, and procedures that have governed institutional teacher evaluation instruments. That means no more lists of teaching behaviors, no more drive-by observations, no more perfunctory pre- and postobservation conferences, and no more signing ceremonies at the end of the school year. The components described below provide a framework for reenvisioning how to make teacher evaluation a more meaningful process.

Goals

The traditional Teacher Evaluation Plan will be replaced with a framework that is designed to accomplish the following goals of professional growth:

- *Relationships:* Professional growth frameworks nurture quality relationships among students, teachers, parents, and administrators.
- *Engagement:* Professional growth frameworks draw teachers into ongoing conversations with colleagues about the practice of teaching.
- *Exploration:* Professional growth frameworks allow teachers to experiment with different ways of teaching.
- *Reflection:* Professional growth frameworks create venues for authoring pedagogies that close the gap between what the research says and what works in classrooms.
- *Focus on Teaching:* Professional growth frameworks focus on what instructional goals teachers intend to accomplish; how teachers organize materials, activities, and subject matter to accomplish intended instructional goals; what tasks students engage in to accomplish intended instructional goals; how teachers treat students; and what student products or performances would demonstrate the accomplishment of, or movement toward, intended instructional goals.
- *Educating:* Professional growth frameworks provide teachers with the time, materials, and expertise to understand and apply increasingly sophisticated approaches to teaching subject matter and close gaps between intended goals for instruction and actual accomplishments of students.

Content

The content of the professional growth framework will not look like a generic list of teaching behaviors nor will it ever become the final documentation of how math or science or reading will be represented in classrooms. Professional growth frameworks are always designed as drafts of what quality teaching looks like for particular subjects that are taught in particular classrooms. For administrative purposes these drafts will be codified at the beginning of each school year. However, a fundamental understanding embedded in professional growth frameworks is the continual editing of what is defined as good teaching based on a continual learning process that transforms "theories of action" (what the research says) into "theories of use" (what actually happens in the classroom) (Argyris & Schön, 1978). Theories in use are finalized interpretations of how a teacher employs craft knowledge to implement a definition of quality teaching in her classroom as essential acts of good teaching:

- *Purpose of Lesson:* The teacher explicitly identifies the relationship between student outcomes (work products) and activity structures. The lesson evidences a clear relationship between previous learning activities and projected learning experiences that will prepare learners for subsequent learning, projects, and performances.
- *Coherent Curriculum:* The teacher develops lessons that establish connections among purposes, subject matter, activities, and student outcomes and demonstrates an understanding of the pedagogical principles that unify a curriculum around essential questions and broad concepts.
- *Discourse Patterns:* The teacher designs activity structures that support the purposes of the lesson and generates discourse patterns that go beyond teacher-talk. Learners engage with each other in purposeful conversations that support inquiry and involve them in practicing the procedures that are important to the discipline and can transfer to problem solving, thinking, and performances.
- *Activity Structures:* The teacher has constructed learning activities that align with the stated targets for learning and that have intellectual integrity. The organization of time, materials, and subject matter reveal a purposeful approach that assists students with methods of inquiry that result in deep understanding of content, advance their communication skills, and promote habits of thinking they can apply in challenging real-world situations. Learning

activities are organized in logical order, building from dependence on the teacher to more independent application. The logic to the sequence should be communicated to students using internal summaries and organizational frameworks that illustrate the relationship between concepts, generalizations, essential questions, facts, and procedures.

- *Representation of Subject Matter:* The teacher has designed a lesson that accurately represents the content, methods, and the kinds of thinking put forth by state content standards and disciplinary experts. The organization and presentation of subject matter evidences high cognitive demand, an emphasis on disciplinary reasoning, and attention to how students understand the subject.
- *Products:* The teacher designs assessments that reflect the purposes of the lesson, accurately represent subject matter understandings, and require the kind of reasoning employed by practitioners in the field of study.

Procedures

Teacher evaluation instruments designed for professional growth discard procedures that focus on documentation of observed and unobserved teaching behaviors with a framework for conducting an ongoing conversation over particular problems or gaps between what a teacher intends to accomplish in the classroom and what students actually produce at the end of a lesson. The instructional reflection consists of a series of conversational moves that elicit from colleagues rich descriptions of how a teacher organized time, materials, subject matter, and activity structures to achieve an intended learning outcome. Figure 6.3 is a graphic representation of the elements in the reflective conversations. The first conversational move consists of listening to individual teachers articulate to supervisors and colleagues the particular instructional goals of a lesson or a series of lessons and how they arranged the time, materials, subject matter, and activity structures to achieve a valued end of schooling.

The second conversational move consists of detailed descriptions by colleagues of what transpired between the teacher and students during the lesson or series of lessons. At no time during this move does the conversation become accusatory or judgmental. The goal of this conversational move is to provide a teacher with a detailed account of how the essential acts of good teaching unfolded in her class.

The third conversational move focuses on gaps in the performance of the essential acts of good teaching. Colleagues participating in this

Figure 6.3   Conversational Moves

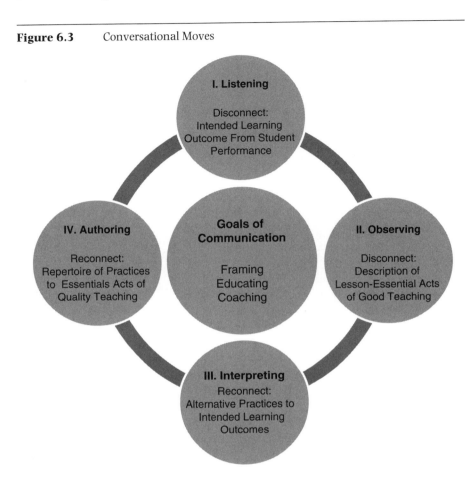

conversational move facilitate a discussion that allows the teacher to identify gaps in the performance of an essential act of good teaching and possible strategies for learning and practicing one or more essential acts of good teaching. The identification of instructional growth goals always originates with the teacher.

Throughout these instructional conversations, colleagues and supervisors always facilitate the instructional conversation from one move to the next move. Colleagues accomplish this role by becoming skilled at the following goals of communication.

Framing means that colleagues assist a teacher with placing his or her perceptions of what is occurring during a lesson within the context of the essential acts of good teaching. The goal of framing is to develop a common vocabulary and establish relationships between essential acts of good teaching and the realities of messy classroom situations.

Educating refers to colleagues offering alternative theories and practices that resolve gaps between intended and actual learning outcomes.

A goal of educating is to develop joint understandings of how to apply theory-driven pedagogies to the essential acts of good teaching.

Coaching means that colleagues assist teachers with constructing instructional strategies that are sensitive to particular classrooms and particular understandings of the essential acts of good teaching.

The final move of the instructional conversation is assisting teachers with authoring an instructional repertoire that merges patterns of teaching that work for them with the essential acts of good teaching. What will emerge out of the conversational mode is not a replication of recommendations from supervisors or colleagues, but rather a personal interpretation of instructional strategies that are faithful to the essentials of quality teaching and make sense to individual teachers.

Professional Development

Any meaningful attempt to use a teacher evaluation system to promote high-quality teaching has to *connect* with curriculum initiatives and professional development. The thread that weaves together all the elements of a coherent approach to curriculum and instruction is the professional development program. The composition of a school's professional development program originates with the gaps that exist between the patterns of instruction that will generate intended instructional outcomes—the essential acts of good teaching—and observed patterns of classroom performance. The ultimate goal of a professional learning culture is continuous learning. Schools that adopt professional learning evaluation instruments closely align their professional development program with gaps in understandings and execution of one or more essential acts of good teaching.

Chapter 5 describes the training regimes that generate deep understandings of the content and implementation of the essential acts of good teaching. The teacher evaluation process becomes the primary source for teachers and supervisors to jointly identify those instructional patterns that warrant a purposeful approach to educating and training staff. The annual professional development program that emerges out of the teacher evaluation process would be an eclectic mix of individualized professional development plans that address a particular instructional pattern of a teacher or a more elaborate program addressing the instructional patterns of teams of teachers, departments, grade levels, or an entire staff. What remains constant in the professional development program is a focus on one or more essential acts of good teaching.

The professional growth framework presented in this chapter is a skeletal version of a teacher evaluation process designed for growing the instructional repertoires of teachers. The flesh of the professional growth plan requires extensive study, discussion, and ultimately, putting on paper a process that places teachers, administrators, and subject matter experts into activity structures that advance the goal of making collective sense out of the implementation of the essential acts of quality teaching. In order for these activity structures to become true centers for professional learning, the configuration of institutional schooling would have to be rearranged in ways that provide teachers with the time, materials, space, and expertise to study, discuss, experiment, and master an essential act of good teaching. In addition to providing the organizational capacity for teachers to willingly take on the difficult task of changing comfortable ways of teaching, administrators must join with teachers in solving instructional problems and assist with the mastery of an essential act of teaching. Administrators who embed themselves in professional growth processes are able to make daily adjustments to schedules, space, materials, and expertise that keep the professional learning process moving forward and send a powerful message to faculty that *teaching matters most.*

The Future of Teacher Evaluation

The professional growth framework presented in this chapter promotes a continuous learning environment where supervisors and teachers collectively deliberate over the meaning and practice of ambitious approaches to teaching and learning. A core value of learning organizations is a trusting culture in which administrators and teachers can openly deliberate, experiment, and practice their craft. While organizational theorists would tell educators that the professional growth framework described in this chapter is our best hope for improving student achievement, national and state governing bodies are mandating that school districts develop evaluation instruments that link teacher performance to student test scores, write procedures that make it easier to dismiss incompetent teachers, and document the rationale for teacher performance ratings. It would appear that for the near future, state legislators will favor institutional approaches to enforcing accountability mandates over models that grow teachers professionally.

School districts that find themselves caught between their belief in professional growth goals and institutional accountability mandates will confront a complex task of finding a middle way between growing teachers professionally and holding teachers accountable for student achievement. School districts that choose to navigate the path between professional growth and accountability should begin that journey with the following principles in mind:

- *Summative and formative procedures for teacher evaluation must be separated.* No teacher will be willing to deliberate, experiment, or reflect on his or her practice in a system that culminates in a rating, a score, or a threat to future employment. Teacher evaluation instruments developed in an era of school accountability must design procedures that separate summative rating systems from the formative process of professional growth. If given the choice by state legislators, school districts should reduce the number of ratings to two (unsatisfactory/satisfactory) and align these ratings with what a district's descriptions of minimum performance of the essential acts of good teaching.

- *Effective teaching behaviors must be understandable and feasible.* Whether a district adopts a growth or accountability-driven teacher evaluation instrument, both approaches must reduce the number of teaching behaviors to the essential acts of good teaching: purposes, representation of subject matter, activity structures, respectful treatment of students and student work products. The long list of teaching behaviors currently on the market may be user-friendly for a checklist mentality, but do not travel well in the messy world of classroom instruction. Teachers understand and are more comfortable with teaching criteria that follow a narrative script: purpose → activities → subject matter → work products. Within this framework, a district can provide more detailed descriptions of what constitutes a worthwhile purpose of instruction, what activities support a school's instructional worldview, what organization of subject matter promotes content standards, and what student work products would evidence the achievement of the lesson goals.

- *Content Matters.* State accountability mandates typically require districts to align their criteria for effective teaching with the ability of the teacher to accurately represent state and national content standards. This means that supervisors with general administrative endorsements will be unable to conduct valid observations of teacher performance. To comply with state mandates to accurately measure teacher performance, supervisors sitting in back of classrooms will be expected to be highly qualified in the subject they are observing.

- *Linking test scores to teacher performance must be marginalized.* The greatest danger to professional growth models is the effort by state legislators to adopt some form of a "value-added" ranking of teachers based on student test scores. School districts can blunt the impact of these value-added mandates by developing a variety of assessments that measure student progress on intended learning outcomes. These assessments would be aligned with essential acts of good teaching. The scores on these assessments would be aggregated in a way that reflects gaps in the schoolwide application of the essential acts of good teaching. A school district would use this gap data as a source for designing the professional development program and school improvement plan. Developing local common assessments and a method of making instructional sense out of the data generated by these assessments may serve as a strategy to meet state mandates to hold teachers accountable for student performance.

SUMMARY

Chapter 6 critiques common models of teacher evaluation that attempt to inspect good teaching in classrooms. We note that a persistent model of teacher evaluation depends on cursory inspections of teachers in classroom and perfunctory conversations that note the presence or absence of instructional features on an adopted checklist. The flaw of these accountability-driven teacher evaluation systems resides with administrators who are too busy managing buildings to devote much time to supervising classroom teaching. Even if they had the time, administrators see a process that has little likelihood of changing teacher behaviors and a great likelihood of lowering faculty morale. We note that while new accountability mandates and models of teacher evaluation are focusing administrators and teachers on the right tasks—classroom instruction—they continue to pursue the wrong goals—assign blame and obtain compliance. As an alternative, we offer a professional growth framework designed to grow a school's definition of good teaching as a recursive process. The details of a teacher evaluation system that emerge out of the professional growth framework are left to administrators and teachers to author. What remains constant in the process of constructing a school's professional growth framework are the three principles for making collective sense out of ambitious approaches to teaching and learning: *coherence* (instructional worldview → essential acts of good teaching); *collaboration* (teacher's identity → essential acts of good teaching); and *concentration* (essential acts of good teaching).

QUESTIONS FOR DISCUSSION AND REFLECTION

1. As you think about the teacher evaluation process you supervise, what is the goal of the process (professional growth or accountability)? Describe components of the evaluation process that support professional growth and those components that serve as obstacles to professional growth.

2. As you think about the classes you have observed, provide an example of effective teaching behavior listed in your plan that teachers often ignore or modify to accommodate the real world of classroom teaching.

3. What changes to your present teacher evaluation plan would have to be made in order to conform to a professional growth framework?

4. As you think about the effective teachers you have observed, describe the essential acts of good teaching they typically employ in their classrooms.

5. If you were to redesign your teacher evaluation plan to align with the goals and substance of a professional growth framework, outline the components of that plan and procedures that you would employ to achieve the goals of a learning organization.

ACTION STEPS FOR TEACHER EVALUATION

→ Review your existing teacher evaluation process and instruments to note how to move the process from a cursory inspection to a more meaningful professional growth model.

→ Form an evaluation team to revise the teacher evaluation model to emphasize professional growth and reflection and to align the evaluation criteria with the local conception of essential acts of good teaching.

→ Plan with other instructional leaders the necessary professional development that will prepare leaders in coaching behaviors and action research models and that will promote the essential acts of good teaching for the whole staff.

Summary of Action Steps

IDENTIFY GAPS BETWEEN STANDARDS AND PERFORMANCES.

INITIATE or RENEW THE FOCUS ON THE QUALITY OF TEACHING.

ASSESS THE EFFECTS ON TEACHING PRACTICES AND ON STUDENT LEARNING.

DEFINE or REDEFINE *QUALITY TEACHING.*

SUPPORT GROWTH THROUGH TEACHER EVALUATION AND COACHING.

HIGH-QUALITY TEACHING

MEASURE and/or REFLECT ON THE CURRENT STATE OF TEACHING.

SUPPORT GROWTH THROUGH A STRATEGIC PLAN OF PROFESSIONAL DEVELOPMENT.

SET GOALS, BUILD ORGANIZATIONAL CAPACITY TO ALIGN EFFORTS.

PROVIDE MEANINGFUL SUPPORT FOR NEW HIRES.

How can we sustain a culture of exceptional instruction?

7

In this book, we have devoted our attention toward helping school leaders to advance the quality of instruction and student satisfaction in schools by suggesting a comprehensive plan to improve the quality of teaching continuously and consistently. We know that it is possible for new or reinvigorated leaders to come on like gangbusters and transform a school into an instructional environment where everyone knows what great teaching looks like and knows the performance standards for every teacher. But how is it possible to sustain the culture of great teaching over time? We recognize that teachers come and go, and various instructional leaders come and go. Many factors affect the consistent quality of teaching in a school, and we would hope that the quality is consistently great. This chapter discusses the observable systems, the common values, and the intangible feeling-tone that contribute to a culture of consistently high-quality instruction.

We list below a set of actions that a school leader should take to sustain high-quality teaching in a school. These actions follow the steps that we describe in the previous chapters: defining high-quality teaching; taking the measure of the state of teaching in a school; recruiting and hiring with the quality standard in mind; providing meaningful induction, mentoring, and professional development experiences aligned with the recognized standard; and following a supportive teacher evaluation program. We list and describe briefly here the efforts toward sustaining quality teaching. In the balance of the chapter, we elaborate about the intention and importance of each measure.

TEN ACTIONS TO SUSTAIN HIGH-QUALITY TEACHING

1. Attend carefully to basic management requirements so that basic routines are unobtrusive, seamless, and practically guaranteed.

2. Minimize distractions to protect the sanctity of the classroom.

3. Set a vision that identifies high-quality teaching as the highest priority in the school.

4. Carefully select the right people for the right positions.

5. Balance leadership between providing direction and giving directives.

6. Communicate in a timely and consistently clear manner.

7. Set the standards for professional conduct, including the way we talk about students and families.

8. Encourage collaborative efforts.

9. Foster reflection and continuous improvement.

10. Engage in ongoing professional dialogues.

SYSTEMS IN PLACE

First, if a school does not have basic systems in place for registration, scheduling, transportation, maintenance, custodial services, food service, attendance reporting, and communication with home, then a principal should drop everything now and turn attention to putting these routine systems in place. The idea is that teachers and students should be able to take certain conditions for granted so that they can turn their complete attention to teaching and learning. It is easy to imagine that teaching is compromised and learning challenged when a radiator whistles in the back of the room, when the classroom swings between blistering heat and arctic chill, when kids miss lunch, when busses don't arrive on time, for instance. This means that the basic systems common to all schools should become routines that only a few people have to think about, and the systems should be in place to support teaching and learning rather than undermine those efforts.

SANCTITY OF THE CLASSROOM

School leaders should do all that they can do to protect the sanctity of the classroom. If someone routinely reads announcements over a public address system, these announcements should be read once a day, at the same time each day. Other announcements should be rare and honor only real emergencies. We know from the research of Hillocks (2009b) that there is a significant negative correlation between classroom diversions and learning—that is, the more diversions, the less learning. By protecting the classroom from the various intrusions that can occur on any day, a school leader sends a signal to everyone that the classroom must be protected because that is where the central business of the school should thrive unimpeded. In some ways, the attention to the seemingly trivial matter of fighting back intrusions is like the police effort to battle the relatively mundane problem of vandalism in an effort to discourage other crimes, the so called "broken windows theory" of Kelling and Coles (1996). Studies have demonstrated that when vandalism, like graffiti and broken windows, is tolerated, other crime emerges because the vandalized areas seem unprotected and vulnerable and the general atmosphere of the community seems to tolerate crime. When we allow a variety of distractions to intrude into the classroom, we admit that instructional time is not terribly valuable. When we keep distractions to a minimum, we signal to everyone that instructional time is a precious commodity and we have to protect it vigilantly.

ENVISIONING QUALITY TEACHING

Taking care of basic management routines and protecting instructional time from distractions implies to everyone that the quality of instruction in a school is most important. But school leaders need to convey explicitly that the highest priority on their agenda is that all students receive high-quality instruction. School leaders can convey this message often, through the conduct of purposeful meetings, the daily interchanges with staff, the written communication to parents, the celebration of accomplishments, the support for professional development, and the reflective conversations with all instructional personnel. *Teaching matters most* should be the mantra and the evaluative filter for judging the merits for various requests, including budget proposals, changes to routine systems, placements for students, or appeals for assemblies and various exceptions to the schedule.

RIGHT PEOPLE IN RIGHT PLACES

If teaching matters most, then personnel decisions are critical. If there are opportunities to place people in leadership and instructional support positions, it is crucial to put the right people in these positions. This requires the discipline to think strategically rather than tactically. By *strategic* we mean acting with special attention to the long-term goals and the honoring of educational values. We have seen leaders work tactically to hire people to befriend an influential person, to invigorate sagging morale, or to address other political expediencies. As an example, we can think about the criteria for hiring an instructional coach, a team leader, or a department head. In making the decision, we would have to ask these questions: What is the candidate's knowledge base? What has been the candidate's experience with students? Does the candidate care about kids? Is the candidate able to communicate effectively? What are the candidate's organizational skills? Generally, what is the basis for making decisions about placing people in positions of leadership? When we begin to make compromises about instructional matters like the hiring of instructional leaders, we undermine our own efforts to advance the quality of teaching. In Resource D, we have included questions for teacher interviews that would be helpful in completing an instructional review, but some of the questions might be useful in screening job candidates.

BALANCED LEADERSHIP

If we have carefully placed people in important leadership positions, this suggests that we have selected people with the appropriate expertise and leadership skills to function in their positions. While we should be able to depend on the expertise of others, it is appropriate for a principal to set a direction for a leadership team. A principal's vision for improving the quality of teaching and the agenda for advancing the instructional program for the school should not be a dark mystery. Every move that a principal makes should be consistent with the goal of advancing the instructional program. When the principal's actions are inconsistent with the explicitly stated vision, everyone recognizes the incongruity and experiences the dissonance. At the same time, the principal should not be directing every move, paralyzing everyone into thinking that individuals cannot act without a specific directive from the principal. Teaching staff should not revert to teaching defensively because they do not know what the principal wants or values. With a clear sense of the underlying principles that support curriculum and drive instruction, teachers should be able to make decisions required for a specific group of students in a specific instructional moment or context. This allowance for a good degree of autonomy recognizes the professional stature of teachers and leaders and satisfies a basic human desire to have some say in decisions that affect them. At the same time, through ongoing dialogue and other means of oversight, a principal can monitor the consistent communitywide effort to improve the quality of teaching continually. The balancing effort includes soliciting and accepting input from a variety of thinkers, without the obligation to act on everyone's suggestions. Seeking input is not the same as promising to honor every request. In brief, principals in schools that sustain efforts toward high-quality teaching practice a kind of balanced leadership, providing direction without giving constant directives and accepting input without committing to every suggestion and without abdicating all decision-making to others.

CLEAR AND TIMELY COMMUNICATION

We recall our first days in graduate programs when we sat in classes with more experienced graduate students who seemed to talk in ways that only they and the professor could understand. They had already been initiated into the esoteric world of graduate studies in a specific discipline. We had to learn to talk the talk. This was part of our induction into the world of graduate studies. We see similar situations occurring in schools, with new teachers trying to figure out a lot of things, including how to talk the way the more experienced staff members talk. School leaders can help to remove the veil of mystery about how we talk about the central goals of the school and the actions in the classroom.

Basic to leadership is the ability to tell the story of where the school has been and to describe where it is going. The principal is most responsible for communicating to instructional staff and to people in leadership positions that the quality of teaching is the highest priority. The principal must make it clear that the highest value is the quality of instruction and the quality of students' experience in the classroom. A school leader can convey this intention and central value in straightforward, nontechnical language. If we talk to our noneducator neighbors and friends and claim that the most important factor to influence the improvement of a school is the quality of teaching, they know on one level exactly what we mean. It seems like common sense. But someone needs to have been in many classrooms and to have engaged in many reflective conversations to say in vivid detail what quality teaching looks like and sounds like. It is also possible to describe these features of instruction in ways that friends, neighbors, and school board members can appreciate. Convenient abbreviations and acronyms seem efficient uses of language, but they can obfuscate meaning and blunt understanding of intent. Straightforward, everyday language should convey goals and shape the image of the kind of school where consistently high-quality teaching is the first priority.

In many ways, leaders have to take back ownership of the language that we use to talk about the mission of schools. We prefer to talk about the *quality of instruction,* the *improvement of learning,* and the *quality of learners' experiences,* as opposed to emphasizing *achievement, improved test scores, metrics, quality dashboards, data mining, data-driven instruction, accountability, interventions,* and *branding*—terms that together seem a strange mix of business and medicine, neither of which represents the central purpose of schools. Principals can give way to the intrusions of this imported language, or they can model and support the language that refers to *children, learners, learning, teaching, supporting, growing,* and *improving.*

It is important to communicate clearly, but it is also important to communicate in a timely manner. Not much frustrates staff and parents more than receiving late notice about decisions and changes that affect the conduct of teaching and learning in the classroom. Principals need to provide for regular and timely communication with staff and parents. It is especially important to communicate regularly with others in instructional leadership positions. One forum for communication is the regular meetings with leaders like department chairs, instructional coaches, and team leaders. We especially like the idea of an annual meeting to review the procedures for teacher evaluation in an effort to reduce misunderstandings about processes and expectations, followed up with regular checks on the progress of the system. We can see value in regular and purposeful meetings with staff members who have a hand in mentoring, developing curriculum, delivering professional development, and supporting classroom activities.

STANDARDS FOR PROFESSIONAL CONDUCT

We recall working together in one high school where the same small group of teachers met over coffee in the teachers' lounge each morning. It didn't take a committed eavesdropper to know that the gist of their conversations recounted their estimation of the despicable behavior of teenagers, the insensitivity of parents, the shortcomings of their colleagues, and the Machiavellian moves of the administrators, which included us. There was almost a tangible dark cloud hovering over their heads. But they were the exception to the whole staff. Over time, with lots of modeling and some correctives, we could move the staff toward embracing more child-centered and learning-centered language and action. The change does not come by way of a memo or an announcement. Instead, over time, as leaders insist on the basic human dignity of all students and all parents and underscore the vast potential for all learners, the same attitude spreads among staff members.

We also recall that over time teachers took pride in working at the school. One teacher observed, "You have to be a pretty good teacher if you continue to work here." That observation derived from the many classroom observations, reflective conversations, department meetings, professional development experiences, and shared readings and discussions that institutionalized the value of high-quality instruction and conveyed the specific criteria that distinguished high-quality teaching. We could see that over time most teachers included some core features of sound instruction: for example, conveying specific goals situated within the context of the preceding lessons and the subsequent lessons, engaging all learners actively and intellectually, attending to formative assessments and self-assessments, aligning assessments with goals and activities, and designing activities that had some intellectual merit. This did not occur all at once, but it took years to realize. If we can indulge in a sports analogy for a moment, we want to refer to the leadership practices of former Bulls and Lakers coach Phil Jackson. In a broadcast of a Bulls game, commentator Stacy King, a former Bulls player, recalled that Jackson emphasized that through practice and repetition the players would develop such strong habits that in times of duress during games, they would rely on the good habits and not fall back on bad habits. This idea is part of what Jackson calls *invisible leadership*. He reached a point with his several championship teams where he did not have to orchestrate every move but could rely on the good habits of others to guide their conduct and decision-making on the court. We judge that in a similar way, with the constant attention to the standards of high-quality instruction, teachers can fall back on good habits, even during the inevitable times of stress and duress.

COLLABORATION

We have seen from our own research (McCann, Ressler, Chambers, & Minor, 2010) the power of teacher collaboration. Lortie's (1975) observations about the characteristic isolation of most teachers remain true today. Most teachers work independently in their own classrooms, with rare visits from teaching colleagues during instructional time. When teachers follow collaborative practices common to lesson study (for example, Stigler & Hiebert, 1999), they focus on the continuous refinement of lessons that attempt to help students learn challenging concepts. In such a collaborative arrangement, teachers plan lessons together, observe each other teach the lessons, refine the lessons, teach again under observation, refine again, and "publish" the resulting highly refined instructional material. The publishing might be as simple as archiving lesson plan documents on a school server or other Internet-accessible server.

In a broader sense, the curriculum that teachers follow should be the product of teachers' work together, even if the curriculum relies heavily on commercially prepared materials. As Marzano (2003) stresses, teachers need to be able to deliver a viable curriculum. To us, this means that the curriculum needs to be more than an oral tradition about what is commonly taught for specific subjects at specific grades, and more than curriculum maps or lists of standards. Teachers need access to bona fide curriculum guides that identify goals, link goals to standards, provide quality instructional materials and plans, and include assessments. School leaders can set the agenda for curriculum development, organize teams to develop and refresh curriculum, provide the necessary professional development about curriculum writing, and monitor and evaluate the process and products.

If teachers are going to move away from isolation and move toward greater collaboration and interdependence, school leaders must provide the time and support to allow teachers to meet together and to observe each other. Teachers commonly report that they crave opportunities to meet with colleagues and that the typical structure of school organizations works against frequent meetings. Providing the time and support for collaboration honors what teachers say they need and fosters their sense of efficacy. Of course, finding meeting time in a crowded school day is a perennial challenge. Realistically, it may take a school leader considerable time to fashion a schedule that is acceptable to teachers, parents, and board members, or to persuade staff members to find their own creative means to work together, either face-to-face or in an online environment. We offer a caution here. Anyone who has attempted to move a staff to work as a professional learning team recognizes that by simply organizing people into groups does not make them productive or even civil teams. The school's professional development plan should foster the communication and group problem-solving practices that help a team to function well.

REFLECTION AND CONTINUOUS IMPROVEMENT

The various aligned efforts in a school, such as induction, mentoring, professional development, curriculum development, and teacher evaluation, should foster reflection and promote a concerted effort for continuous improvement. Ideally, we would like to see each teacher in a school attempting every day to teach the perfect lesson, for its own sake. Perhaps that sounds too idealistic, and we recognize that no one will actually attain perfection. But we judge that teachers and school leaders define for themselves the quality of their own experience. There are certainly external factors in any school day or class period that affect our experience, but there are also internal factors, like fatigue, doubt, loss of concentration, wavering commitment, to name a few. In contrast to popular conceptions, we judge that teachers can measure their *daily* performance against a perfection standard, as opposed to looking back on the previous *year's* performance through the lens of the achievement test scores for students who have already moved on to the next grade. We understand that illness, bereavement, economic peril, and other sources of stress will interfere with a teacher's best efforts. But the mentoring, professional development, and teacher evaluation systems should promote a culture of striving toward an ideal. Every day, the media will include stories that imply or overtly express doubt about the performance and commitment of teachers. In contrast, the local school leaders should promote and celebrate the idea that *teaching matters most* and that all teachers should strive to do their best every day. This is what defines a teacher.

If we can indulge in another sports analogy, we will recall our days as rather mediocre tennis players. Although it didn't turn our games around dramatically, we came under the influence of Gallwey's *The Inner Game of Tennis* (1986). In Gallwey's descriptions, we recognized in ourselves the various mind games we played while competing in tennis—"Since it is already 30-love, I'll concede this point and then I'll get the serve back to have a chance to win a game." "I hope, I hope, I hope he double faults." "I think a cramp is developing in my left knee, which will allow me to explain my poor play."—and so on. In contrast, if we concentrated on the moment—hitting a sweet serve, returning a serve with authority, hitting the backhand where we wanted it—the end result—winning the game— would take care of itself. In fact, the quality of our experience as tennis players depended on being in the moment to strive for that perfect shot, for the sake of the beauty of accomplishing that ideal, or at least coming near. Gallwey drew heavily from Zen thinkers, and his popular tennis book led to other spin-offs, including *The Inner Game of Work* (Gallwey, 2001). In a sense, we were trying to experience the Zen or phenomenology of tennis. We judge that with the vision and support of leaders who emphasize the quality of teachers' and learners' experiences every day, teachers can experience the Zen of teaching, with each day a striving for perfection. Every day we emerge from classrooms with a sense of how close we came to the ideal we wanted to achieve. We might think, "That discussion went well, although I still haven't heard much from the guy in the corner who seems apathetic. Next time, I think I will initiate discussion by soliciting his thoughts." The seemingly simple reflection suggests that the teacher strives toward a truly dialogic classroom and values the participation of all class members as necessary for the shared inquiry. If the lesson has fallen short, the teacher does not despair but thinks of adjustments to move practice closer to the ideal. The striving toward the ideal defines the quality of experience.

ONGOING PROFESSIONAL DIALOGUES

Principals and other school leaders need to talk shop almost incessantly in school. They need to engage with others in ongoing professional dialogues. Of course, there is a danger that a principal can initiate conversation in an accusatory way, for example, "Are you still relying on those insipid word search worksheets?" If someone is going to make a dialogic bid (Nystrand, 1997), she will need to frame the inquiry in such a way that it suggests a common understanding and recognizes the knowledge of the other participants—"I know that you have worked hard to refresh the geometry curriculum to make it more project-based. How has that worked out? How are kids responding?" The difference in the latter example is that the principal initiating the conversation recognizes that the geometry teacher has done some important curriculum work, and she appreciates that the teacher is reflective enough to evaluate the impact of the curriculum changes. The way that the principal introduces and frames the question makes all the difference. When the conversational partners build from such a positive inquiry frame, the conversation is likely to remain constructive, contribute to a positive and professional tone throughout the building, and underscore the importance of the work of the teachers in the school. Having such conversations in hallways, in the teachers' lounge, in the parking lot, and in meeting rooms should be commonplace and convey the idea that the shared interest of the principal and staff of the school is that students are receiving the best instruction possible and having the best possible experience in the classroom.

To follow the recommendations from this chapter, a principal would have to attend seriously to his or her own professional development by reading extensively, attending selected conferences, and conferring with colleagues. The principal's influential readings can find their way into the lives of teachers and can become the focus for discussions. The idea is not to hold seminars about the principal's reading list, with the principal dominating the discussions. Instead, the experience of sharing literature about teaching and learning is a given for teams of professionals who embrace the idea that teaching matters most and strive together to make the quality of instruction and the quality of students' experience every day as meaningful and compelling as possible.

SUMMARY

In this chapter, we offer recommendations for sustaining a school culture that conveys the value that *teaching matters most*. Many factors can undermine efforts to maintain high-quality teaching, but a few common-sense efforts can help to push back the pressures that threaten to diminish the growth of a staff. The efforts include attention to the goals that one sets and the language that one uses to talk about students, parents, and the endeavors of schools. Principals convey the values they hold not only by how they speak, but also by the actions they take. We urge an effort to minimize distractions and to promote collaboration. Taken together, the various recommendations should foster reflective practice and perhaps allow teachers to experience the Zen or inner game of teaching. Responsibility falls to the principal to attend to his or her own professional development, to set an example, and to inform moves designed to advance the quality of instruction.

QUESTIONS FOR DISCUSSION AND REFLECTION

1. What are the basic systems that your school has in place to register students, take attendance, collect grades, deliver lunches, transport students, communicate with teachers, and so forth? How are these systems working? To what extent are any of these systems compromised to the point that they make the work of teaching more difficult than it has to be? What can you do to repair or refine the systems?

2. If you were to complete a kind of audit of the kinds of distractions that can interfere with the quality of teaching and learning every day, what would you find? What steps could you take to suppress or minimize the distractions?

3. What is your sense about the prevailing feeling tone and dominant language in your school? How do teachers talk about kids and their parents? What can you do to influence the talk in school to move it to a higher professional level?

4. How well do you communicate with staff? What is the basis for your judgment? If others could speak candidly to you, what would they recommend that you do to refine your communication practices?

5. What opportunities do you provide for teachers to collaborate? Are these rare occasions, like summer curriculum projects, or regular

occurrences? What can you do to facilitate teacher's collaborating on a regular basis? What value do you see in the collaborations?

ACTION STEPS TO FOSTER A CULTURE OF HIGH-QUALITY TEACHING

→ Take action to minimize classroom intrusions and to protect the sanctity of the classroom. This action should affect public address announcement and in-school systems for communicating with teachers and students.

→ Examine your existing daily schedule to find times when teachers can meet to collaborate. The schedule is the beginning point. You will also need to encourage collaborative efforts for planning and for reflections on the effects of instruction. A move to a more collaborative environment requires the professional development needed to foster productive teamwork.

→ Prepare an individual professional growth plan that will advance your expertise about the classroom practices that most effectively promote students' learning and satisfaction. Your plan should include attention to how you will share what you have learned with other members of the staff and engage them in dialogue about this learning.

Summary of Action Steps

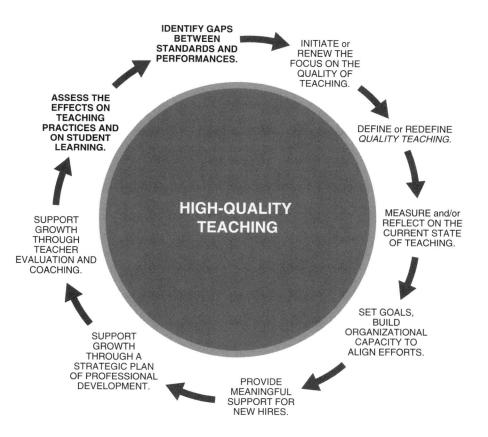

IDENTIFY GAPS BETWEEN STANDARDS AND PERFORMANCES.

INITIATE or RENEW THE FOCUS ON THE QUALITY OF TEACHING.

DEFINE or REDEFINE *QUALITY TEACHING.*

MEASURE and/or REFLECT ON THE CURRENT STATE OF TEACHING.

SET GOALS, BUILD ORGANIZATIONAL CAPACITY TO ALIGN EFFORTS.

PROVIDE MEANINGFUL SUPPORT FOR NEW HIRES.

SUPPORT GROWTH THROUGH A STRATEGIC PLAN OF PROFESSIONAL DEVELOPMENT.

SUPPORT GROWTH THROUGH TEACHER EVALUATION AND COACHING.

ASSESS THE EFFECTS ON TEACHING PRACTICES AND ON STUDENT LEARNING.

HIGH-QUALITY TEACHING

How do we face our leadership challenges?

8

When colleagues and family members have read various drafts of this book, they expressed a similar reaction: "This seems like such common sense. Why aren't schools doing this now?" The simple answer is that moving forward with a concerted plan to advance the quality of teaching in a school requires some leadership skills that not everyone shares. While the plan is rather straightforward, with truths hidden in plain view, we recognize that any plan to improve schools will meet some significant challenges. This chapter recognizes the realistic challenges and describes the leadership practices that offer the hope to move an improvement plan forward.

Every school will have its unique complex of resources, strengths, and challenges. When we have described to others our plan for school improvement, with its emphasis on advancing the quality of teaching, we have heard some common cautions across the several commentators. We address the most frequently identified cautions under five categories:

1. *Distractions.* The principal might want to focus most energy on improving the quality of instruction, but other distractions intrude, especially directed by central office administrators.

2. *Principals' Knowledge.* Some principals have little experience as classroom teachers themselves and have only superficial knowledge about the work that teachers do and about the elements that define quality teaching.

3. *Lack of Trust.* A skeptical staff might view a renewed emphasis on teacher quality with suspicion, inferring an agenda of aggressive removal of targeted staff.

4. *Teachers' Resistance.* For a variety of reasons, teachers may resist, or fail to benefit from, mentoring, coaching, and professional development.

5. *Slow Change.* For a principal pressured to show immediate results, the prospect of following a slow and steady plan toward consistent improvement of instruction will seem unlikely to satisfy an ambitious superintendent or impatient school board.

SUPPRESSING DISTRACTION

We have worked under the direction of superintendents and school boards who had interest in a variety of school initiatives, including exotic grading schemes, creative scheduling, widespread data collection and analysis, building beautification, boosting staff morale, cutting operations costs, curriculum mapping, community partnerships, and ramping up test scores, to name a few. We have to admit that none of these initiatives in and of themselves is bad. But we can see how a principal can become distracted and spread energies too thinly in attempting to address myriad demands all at once. We also worry about a preoccupation with any one of the initiatives distracting the principal away from close attention to improving the quality of instruction. Take curriculum mapping, for example. We recognize the value in the alignment and mapping of the curriculum so that the arrangement of the learning experiences makes sense as a coherent whole and so that staff members across the school have access to and awareness of the various components of the curriculum. At the same time, we do not see how curriculum mapping will overcome weak or uneven teaching, even though in many instances the curriculum mapping in itself appears as an antidote to weak teaching. We assess other initiatives similarly; there is no harm in following them, until they distract from the core mission of the school to advance the learning and positive experience of students.

Chapter 3 of this book offers an outline for a rationale to present to a school board or to central office administrators to explain why any emphasis on the comprehensive improvement in the quality of teaching is important. We recommend a review of the outline, referral to the support that we cite, and practice in making the case to peers, friends, or neighbors. We have always held to the idea that if we couldn't make sense to our noneducator neighbors, we were unlikely to persuade school board members and a superintendent. The vision of improving a school through a relentless emphasis on the improvement in the quality of teaching must be perfectly clear in order to garner support and push back distractions.

Moving forward with the support of the superintendent and school board will make life easier. If, however, it is necessary to mine data, map the curriculum, construct "quality dashboards," for instance, we see no harm in honoring those efforts, unless they distract the principal from the core business of schools—to deliver consistently high-quality instruction. A typical challenge that principals everywhere face is managing several responsibilities and responding to several demands almost simultaneously. So the juggling of the more peripheral initiatives while keeping close attention on advancing the quality of teaching is a realistic possibility. The key is that the principal is able to distinguish the peripheral from the essential, and can set priorities in such a way that everyone in the school knows that fidelity toward continuously improving the quality of teaching is the first obligation.

BUILDING THE PRINCIPAL'S KNOWLEDGE

On several occasions, we have expressed to teachers that our vision for improving schools depends on a principal's relentless effort to improve the quality of teaching. A few times experienced teachers have responded to our plan with a derisive guffaw and a comment that sounds something like this: "You've got to be kidding. My principal wouldn't know good teaching if he met it on the street. How is he going to coach me to become a better teacher?" At first, this commentary takes us aback because we have high regard for some fine principals who have long experience in the classroom and are as credible as teachers as they are as principals. But we have to admit to knowing some principals who we have a hard time seeing as instructional leaders. In some instances, their teaching background is quite limited or their experience in school was in a specialist role or a nonteaching capacity. These leaders have some work to do to build credibility with a faculty.

In Chapter 2 we suggest some features of quality teaching. While we appreciate that all teaching is contextualized, we judge that there are some features of good teaching that should cross all boundaries. You don't have to be a curriculum expert or a subject area specialist to know that teaching is better when the teacher is able to manage a class productively through a positive rapport with students. Explicitly stated or easily inferred goals help to focus learning, logically sequenced activities with smooth transitions support learning more than disjointed lesson episodes, and intellectually engaging activities prompt better outcomes than do routine recitations and worksheets. Luckily, there is a vast body of literature that describes the features of high-quality instruction. The sources we cite in Chapter 2 can serve as a beginning point for a principal who needs to think about the qualities that separate distinguished teachers from mediocre teachers and to develop the language for talking about these features.

Most parents think that they can readily judge who are the better teachers and the weaker teachers in a school. To a certain extent their judgments are reliable. But life in the classroom is complicated, as several researchers, including Lortie (1975), Jackson (1986), and Kennedy (2005) have demonstrated. A deep understanding of the nature of the task of teaching requires more than being able to recite the criteria from a teacher evaluation rubric. The demand for any principal is to immerse him- or herself deeply in the literature about teaching in order to have thorough insight and deep appreciation for the work that teachers do. A principal needs to invest in his or her own professional development by learning more and more about the life of the classroom. This recommendation extends to anyone who works in a supervisory capacity under the direction of the principal, including assistant principals, department heads, or other directors who have a hand in teacher evaluation and professional development. If the principal has a team of supervisors, this team should meet regularly and discuss how they see the quality of teaching advancing, or stagnating, if that is the case.

BUILDING TRUST

A skeptical faculty might well be suspicious of a principal's sudden interest in advancing the quality of teaching. In those cases where there is already substantial distrust, the challenge to build trust will be substantially more difficult. One should begin by considering the elements that foster trust in any relationship. If trust develops, it typically develops over time, after several shared experiences when the agents in the relationship have demonstrated themselves to be trusting and trustworthy. In general, trust derives from honesty, openness, candor, fidelity, and to a certain extent, vulnerability.

In Chapter 3, we suggest a process for working with a faculty to define quality teaching. The process should begin with an open expression of the agenda for school improvement. How a principal expresses the agenda is critical. Consider, for example, the contrast between the two statements below:

1. Principal Hardimann: We have reached a point where we can no longer tolerate lackluster teaching. Going forward, everyone has to improve his or her teaching. I am going to lay out my expectations, and I will be visiting classrooms frequently to see that everyone is accountable in measuring up to the standard.

2. Principal Rogers: For all of the school improvement efforts we might pursue in any school year, I recognize that improvement depends almost entirely on the good work that you do in the classroom. And I understand that as professionals, you are always interested in advancing the quality of instruction. This year we are going to join together in defining what quality instruction is, and we will provide the resources that you need in refining your craft as teachers.

We hope that the reader will agree with us in concluding that the first statement expresses skepticism, if not outright disrespect; and the response from teachers is likely to be distrust and defensiveness. The second statement might sound a bit like pandering to an audience, but it expresses what we honestly judge to be the truth about what matters most in schools. The statement offers a positive supposition—that we understand that teachers are at the heart of the school's mission, that they do good work, and that as professionals, they will want to refine their craft continuously. But the opening statement is not enough to foster and sustain trust. The principal will have to stay true to a collaborative process in order to arrive at the shared expression of what high-quality teaching is. We caution, though, that collaboration and deliberation does not mean that all ideas in the end are honored. The process must lead to a synthesis of the components of high-quality teaching, evaluated against what the research reveals about the kind of instruction that promotes learning and fosters student satisfaction. And the principal will need to follow through with any promise to deliver the support—for mentoring, meaningful professional development, cognitive coaching, and curriculum renewal. Mutual trust of the sort that will allow a faculty to move forward in an attempt to improve the quality of teaching without being threatened by the effort requires the principal to follow through with the agenda and with the promise for support. The principal will have to resist the prevailing rhetoric in political arenas and popular media that conveys a sense of skepticism about teachers, which is an attitude that compromises trust. Instead, the principal has to embrace the idea that teachers prefer to be competent at what they do, work hard, and mean to do their best for students and parents.

INFLUENCING RESISTANT TEACHERS

According to Mary M. Kennedy (2005), teachers seem to be "immune" (p. 2) to efforts at school reform. Kennedy's study reveals the complexity of events in the classroom and accounts in great detail for teachers' thinking about what they do and why they do it. Given Kennedy's findings, it would not be surprising if a principal's attempt at advancing the quality of teaching in a school met some resistance, or the principal had the feeling that the faculty members "just don't get it." We offer here some suppositions about quality instruction; and drawing from Kennedy's study in part, we account for possible resistance. We also suggest how the concerted efforts across the school, for example, mentoring, coaching, and professional development, might expand thinking about teaching and help teachers to cope with situations that seem to threaten the tranquility in their classrooms.

Our understanding of quality teaching envisions instruction that students find intellectually engaging, if not invigorating. As we note in Chapter 2, practices that some consider to be effective or competent teaching might emphasize that students are quietly working in their seats, the teacher is covering content, and learners are preparing adequately for achievement tests. We see such classrooms falling far short of a standard for quality instruction. Our vision, built on the research in the several studies we cite at the beginning of Chapter 3, sees students actively engaged and cognitively invested in the learning activities in the classroom. One of our university students noted as a general standard, "Teach no lesson that you could just as well teach with no students present" (P. Dalton, personal communication, April 1, 2010). This means that students have to be involved, especially through interactions with the teacher and with their peers. A teacher who turns on the DVD and directs students to fill in a worksheet, or the teacher who advances presentation slides and reads aloud the bullet points may have a quiet and orderly classroom, but is not challenging learners to think critically and creatively, to develop a deep understanding of the big concepts of a discipline, to practice complex communication, to solve ill-structured problems, or to work collaboratively with others. Certainly there is a place for presentation, recitation, and quiet seatwork, but these experiences should not dominate and define the life of the classroom.

Kennedy (2005) notes that teachers follow general scripts that direct the activities of lessons, and teachers fight back distractions that might compromise the scripts. This battle against the threat of distractions can undermine the students' intellectual engagement.

> The most important finding revealed in this chapter is that intellectual engagement can significantly *add* to teachers' difficulties, and that as a result teachers frequently discourage intellectual engagement. Just as students who are disengaged can disrupt lessons by misbehaving, so can students who are engaged disrupt lessons by enthusiastically offering ideas that move the lesson away from the direction teachers are aiming for. (p. 29)

Kennedy's descriptions remind us of the missed opportunities we have witnessed when active inquiry turned to quiet submission, where authentic discussion diminished to recitation.

We are asking a lot from teachers, not in the sense of piling on work for them, but possibly by expecting them to reimagine their practices and routines in the classroom. We recognize that the kind of instruction that calls for active learning and lots of peer interaction is likely to pose a threat to many teachers. The kind of inquiry-based learning that Dewey (1938) envisioned long ago required that the teacher introduce *doubt* in order to initiate investigation through a deliberate and strategic means. Vygotsky (1986) cites Jean-Jacques Rousseau, who describes moments when "the mind bumps up against the wall of its own inadequacy." These moments represent the opportunities for learning, as learners attempt to reconcile preconceived notions with new experiences, information, and challenges. Functioning in an area of *doubt* can be both stimulating and unsettling, for students and teachers alike. Teachers will need to see for themselves through demonstrations and other professional development opportunities how one can introduce and build from moments of doubt, how one can transcend recitation and move toward discussion, deliberation, and collaboration, and how one can emphasize transferable procedures instead of simple recall. Stephens et al. (2000) remind us that one is not likely to fixate the beliefs that guide action because someone *told* you that something was so. Instead, it is through the process of inquiry and discovery that one develops the firmly held beliefs about how learners learn and about how teachers can most effectively teach. These beliefs in turn guide actions.

One leadership responsibility for the principal then is to provide for teachers the kind of meaningful professional development opportunities that engage them in inquiry processes and reveal how to function in classroom situations when the deviations from the script threaten and when intellectual engagement can lead to a productive sequence rather than a fruitless digression. In their observations and related conversations, principals need to help teachers to reflect on classroom planning and decisions and explore options that would move narrowly scripted teaching to episodes of sustained intellectual engagement. Again, observing carefully and facilitating planning and reflective conversations requires some skills on the part of the principal and other supervisors who are involved in the process of coaching teachers. Minimally, the skills include framing the inquiry delicately, listening carefully, paraphrasing and clarifying reliably, and describing and evaluating options clearly and succinctly. If a principal or other supervisors working directly with teachers in classrooms do not have highly refined skills at coaching others, they should seek training and other opportunities for practice to refine skills.

By the very nature of the position as instructional leader in a school, a principal will have to be a generalist, responsible for quality teaching in all subjects. Realistically, the principal will not be a content expert for every discipline. This is especially an issue in middle school and high school. To complicate matters further, teachers from various disciplines do not think of their subjects, curriculum, and teaching in the same way (Grossman & Stodolsky, 1995; Stodolsky & Grossman, 1995). In other words, science teachers and English teachers are not interchangeable; they have distinct ways they think about knowledge, curriculum, and how learners should learn the concepts in their disciplines. Again, this does not mean that each principal needs to be a content expert for every subject. Instead, principals need to know a good deal about basic principles for curriculum; they also need to select and rely on knowledgeable subject specialists to help teachers to advance teaching within their own discipline. As we point out in Chapter 7, to have a reliable team of specialists to support the broad endeavor to advance the quality of teaching in all subjects, a principal will have to have specific and relevant selection criteria in mind and make disciplined decisions about putting the right people in the right places.

Another supposition we offer is that teachers cannot facilitate lessons that are intellectually engaging and that rely on high levels of purposeful peer interaction unless the teachers are working with a coherent curriculum. Teachers and learners are at a distinct disadvantage when goals are uncertain, assessments unaligned with goals, and lessons disjointed. In many cases, the quality of the teaching will reveal the quality of the curriculum. We understand that everything in a school is ultimately part of the curriculum, but for our current purposes, we refer to the content, materials, learning activities, and assessments as the basic elements in the curriculum. A deep understanding of specific disciplines leads to the development of tangible goals, often defined by the assessments that express the overt behaviors that reveal skills and understandings. Part of the challenge for the principal as instructional leader is to assess the state of the curriculum, judge the extent to which the curriculum supports or inhibits teachers, and initiate and organize curriculum renewal projects where they are needed.

In high schools and in some middle schools, the department heads typically lead the curriculum review and renewal effort. But we would not take for granted that teachers have a good intuitive sense of how to develop curriculum. Preparation for curriculum renewal projects should involve training in a curriculum construction model. Wiggins and McTighe's (2005) influential work is a logical starting point for guidance in systematically developing a curriculum.

COPING WITH THE PACE

If there is significant room for growth in the quality of teaching in a school, the pace for seeing significant change will likely be slow. Certainly what we recommend throughout this book is not a quick fix. We have not seen overnight transformations of schools that rely on devices that promise to boost academic achievement immediately. We fear that instead the pressures for a quick turn-around leads to the kind of abuses that affected Atlanta public schools, where scores of administrators and teachers faced punitive action for falsifying assessments (Severson, 2011). The familiar analogy is that the process of turning around an ocean liner will necessarily be slow. It is not like maneuvering a small sports car through a U-turn. If there is room in the school for significant growth, realistically the process will take awhile. Consider that the process involves garnering support from leadership, building trust among staff, deriving a common standard for quality teaching, seeking teachers who meet the standard, imparting the standard to new staff, providing for reliable mentoring, planning for meaningful professional development for teachers and supervisors, reviewing curriculum, and managing a supportive teacher evaluation program. As we note in Chapter 7, it is too early to begin these efforts until basic systems are already in place in the school.

The list of responsibilities may seem daunting, but they are likely to be part of a principal's job description already. The difference might be that the principal who makes a difference in advancing the quality of teaching in a school is someone who takes all these responsibilities seriously and sets priorities in such a way that it is clear to everyone that at the core of all efforts is the advancement of teaching and learning.

FINAL THOUGHTS

We have tried to be realistic about the possible challenges in trying to advance the quality of teaching across all subjects and all grades in a school. Any experienced educator could probably predict several more challenges. But we remain hopeful, and even enthusiastic, that school leaders can make a difference by focusing most attention on what happens in the classroom. We have visited many schools and sat in many classrooms where we were disappointed in the quality of instruction and saddened at the implied low expectations and the apparent lack of intellectual engagement and the flat experience for kids. The saddest part for us is that the situation did not have to be this way. We saw students prepared for learning in schools that had abundant resources and intelligent, well-meaning teachers. Perhaps the missing element for teachers was the instructional leadership that would place a premium on high-quality teaching and provide the vision and support to help all teachers to refine their craft for their own professional satisfaction and for the benefit of all learners.

SUMMARY

This chapter acknowledges that the path to significant improvement in the quality of teaching can be difficult, but the series of chapters in this book lays out an aligned plan for advancing the quality of instruction in a school. In the chapter, we note the possibility of some significant challenges facing leaders who attempt to follow through with the plan: suppressing distractions, building knowledge about teaching, building trust, influencing resistant teachers, and tolerating the slow pace of change. We see hope beyond these potential obstacles, and we suggest what is needed to contend with the challenges. In the end, the hope for teachers and for students is a renewal of teaching that engages all learners intellectually and guarantees a quality experience for all learners.

QUESTIONS FOR DISCUSSION AND REFLECTION

1. What are the potential diversions that could derail a plan to focus on advancing the quality of teaching across a school? What are the other initiatives within your school or district? How can you coordinate these other initiatives so that they support your focus on the quality of teaching?

2. How would you characterize the level of trust between the principal and faculty in your school? What are the specific steps you can take to foster further trust with the faculty?

3. What is the status of the curriculum in your school? Where does the curriculum need further development? What are the priorities? Where would you start, and how would you progress in a strategic way to attend to the curriculum needs in all areas? How would you provide for the professional development that logical curriculum development requires?

4. If you were to assess your own preparedness to observe and assess classroom practices and conduct the kind of reflective conversations that will foster professional growth, what do you need to

advance your own skills to conduct these important activities? What are your specific plans for your own professional growth as an expert about quality teaching?

5. If you can't be an expert in every subject, who are the people you can rely on to collaborate in the plan to advance the quality of teaching in a way that is specific to certain disciplines? How will you sustain communication with these other experts to maintain focus and assess advancement?

ACTION STEPS FOR FACING LEADERSHIP CHALLENGES

→ Take a candid inventory of the local challenges that you can expect to encounter in an attempt to foster a culture of high-quality teaching and fashion a plan for facing those challenges.

→ Identify and communicate with curriculum specialists for specific disciplines and share with them your long-term commitment to improving the quality of teaching and describe their roles in the process.

→ Considering other initiatives that seem to be important in your school district, plan a strategy to honor those initiatives while keeping the goal of consistent high-quality teaching the highest priority.

Summary of Action Steps

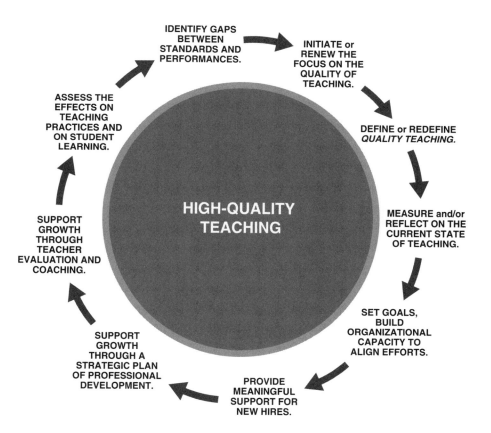

IDENTIFY GAPS BETWEEN STANDARDS AND PERFORMANCES.

INITIATE or RENEW THE FOCUS ON THE QUALITY OF TEACHING.

ASSESS THE EFFECTS ON TEACHING PRACTICES AND ON STUDENT LEARNING.

DEFINE or REDEFINE *QUALITY TEACHING.*

HIGH-QUALITY TEACHING

SUPPORT GROWTH THROUGH TEACHER EVALUATION AND COACHING.

MEASURE and/or REFLECT ON THE CURRENT STATE OF TEACHING.

SUPPORT GROWTH THROUGH A STRATEGIC PLAN OF PROFESSIONAL DEVELOPMENT.

SET GOALS, BUILD ORGANIZATIONAL CAPACITY TO ALIGN EFFORTS.

PROVIDE MEANINGFUL SUPPORT FOR NEW HIRES.

Resource A

How Can You Spot a Really Good Teacher?

(Discussed in Chapter 3)

Inquiry Frame: With one or two colleagues, decide which of the following teachers appears to be someone who *you would want to teach at your school.* Note what influenced your decision. If you rejected someone, why doesn't he or she fit the image of the kind of teacher you would like to see in your school? If you judge that someone has the *potential for being a good teacher,* describe the *characteristics* that influenced your selection. You might choose that several teachers are good teachers, even though they have different pedagogical styles. The important goal of your inquiry is to define the kind of teacher that we would like to represent a school where you teach.

GLIMPSES OF SIX TEACHERS

1. Stanislaus Lindner is an avid reader and a meticulous planner. He spends a great deal of time planning lectures for his class. Although he has taught the same subject for a number of years, he is aware of the need to keep his lectures current and fresh. Mr. Lindner is very knowledgeable about his discipline. He has published widely on a variety of subjects in his discipline. Professional organizations and other schools have frequently invited Mr. Lindner to be a speaker at workshops and conferences. Mr. Lindner has told colleagues, "You need to connect the material to the knowledge and world of the students. I am careful to begin each class by

giving students some kind of outline for the lesson. The outline offers a preview and gives students a framework for processing the information. This strategy is what David Ausebel calls an 'advanced organizer.'" Mr. Lindner also understands that students like to relate the abstract and unfamiliar to the experiences in their own everyday world. Mr. Lindner then provides graphic analogies to illustrate the concepts in his lecture. He also has a sense of the dramatic. He structures his lectures to provide surprises and to challenge students to think about their assumptions in a new light. Mr. Lindner's classes are very orderly. Students have no doubt about his objectives and his expectations. He sets a clear agenda and provides structures for students to follow and conform.

Mr. Lindner is also skillful at conducting large group discussions. He involves everyone in his discussions. His manner is truly Socratic. He poses a general question and allows someone to respond. He then calls on other students to evaluate the speaker's observations. He extends discussion by asking students to explain or defend their positions. He is marvelously inventive in citing some example to challenge the universality of a student's claim. Through the process of careful questioning and probing, Mr. Lindner helps students to clarify their notions and prepares them to defend their points of view.

2. Brendan Carmody hoped to expose his history students to an experience that would allow them to discover the stratification of medieval European society. Although he worried that the sacrifice of instructional time might make it difficult for him to cover the target material for the first semester, he devoted two days to allowing students to learn and play the game of chess. Mr. Carmody had recruited eight chess "experts" from among his class. Each "expert" met with two other students to teach them the rudiments of how to play the game. After the pairs of students were sufficiently comfortable with the basic rules and strategies of the game, they faced off to play the game in earnest. At the beginning of the lesson on the next day, Mr. Carmody directed the students to take out their journals and write a one-paragraph response to the following question: How does the game of chess symbolically represent the stratification of medieval European society? Mr. Carmody allowed the students ten minutes to record their observations. When he called on volunteers to report their observations, Mr. Carmody judged their responses to be uninformed and misguided. Exasperated, he berated the students: "What's the matter with you people? Don't you get it?" He then directed the students to take out their notes and record his observations as he dictated "Eight Characteristics of Medieval European Society." When a few students grumbled, Mr. Carmody noted: "Hey, this is important! It's going to be on the test next week."

3.   Justin Duer believes learning must be active. He wants to involve the students in their learning. Justin has reflected that the times when he has achieved the deepest understanding of the content of his subject has been when he has had to teach it to someone else. He reasoned that it follows logically that students will also reach a deep understanding if they assumed the role of teacher. He has designed what he sees as his defining lesson for teaching ninth graders in his world geography class about cultures of the Middle East. He assigns each of six small groups of students particular nations to study. Each expert group has to prepare notes about the predominant religion of the nation, the economic system, the system of government, the features of the physical geography, and prime examples of the distinctive art of that nation. Each student has to research an assigned topic, record key facts on note cards, and prepare and rehearse a brief presentation. Justin then reserves the school's large multipurpose room, where he sets up makeshift tents to simulate a Middle Eastern bazaar. Each tent represents a different nation. Justin encourages the students to come to class on the designated day wearing the appropriate simulated clothing of the nation they represent. The dynamic part of the activity requires students to take turns in traveling from tent to tent to hear the presentations and take notes on the structured note pages that Justin provides. Each tent dweller takes a turn in presenting and makes at least three circuits around the bazaar to collect information. Justin has taken pictures of these events and has posted them on the class website for students and parents to enjoy. The students later take a comprehensive exam on the information on all of the nations represented at the bazaar. To Justin's mind, the beauty of the activity is that students learn from students.

4.   Olga Mater knows kids. She raised five of her own. She stayed home to raise her children, but when they grew older and more independent, Mrs. Mater (and she prefers *Mrs.*) returned to teaching. In watching her own children face the difficulties posed by school and peers, she witnessed many challenges to her children's self-esteem. As she returned to the classroom, Mrs. Mater promised herself that her primary role was that of protector of the spirit and value of each student. She sees her classroom as a little community. At the beginning of each day, she recites this prayer: "Let my life be a model to others/That the child may become the person/That the person may become the citizen/That the citizen may become the spirit /That enriches the life of the world." Mrs. Mater follows the school's recommended curriculum, yet she places less value on cognitive development and more on affective development. She reasons that when a child feels good about herself, she is likely to learn; when a child feels low, she is incapable of learning.

Mrs. Mater consistently assigns brief homework assignments. She recognizes that the child's time at home with family and friends is very important. She sees no point in assigning lengthy tasks that will frustrate and exhaust the students. She makes most assignments simple enough for everyone in the class to be successful. And she rewards success in many ways. She provides stickers, candy, and bookmarks as acknowledgements for work well done. In one corner of the classroom, Mrs. Mater has positioned an overstuffed chair and ottoman that her husband and eldest son have dragged into the school. Every Friday in Mrs. Mater's class is sharing day. She selects certain students to share with the class the best work that they have completed during the week. The student ascends to the overstuffed chair, which Mrs. Mater likes to refer to as the "throne," and rests comfortably while explaining what he has accomplished or while reading something he has written or read.

Most lessons in Mrs. Mater's class are predictable. She begins by listing the lesson objectives on the board. She briefly describes the lesson activities. Mrs. Mater conducts the lesson for a time through presentation, modeling, or demonstration. She then assigns the students a brief task. As the students work independently, Mrs. Mater checks their work and provides feedback, usually in the form of positive comments. When Mrs. Mater recognizes that the students can function without her assistance, she makes an assignment that the students can begin in class and complete for homework.

Mrs. Mater occasionally relies on cooperative learning activities. In forming groups, she tries to create teams that will allow everyone to contribute. She doesn't want anyone's voice to be suppressed. Mrs. Mater closely watches the behavior in each group. Sometimes she changes the group membership when she sees that the dynamics are negative. One example reveals her typical approach to discipline problems: A student who recently returned from hospitalization for drug rehabilitation ridicules another student in his group for being a "Bible-beating wetback." Mrs. Mater was appalled. She did not publicly berate the insensitive student. Instead, she stopped all other activity in the lesson, saying, "We cannot continue our study of periodic sentences when one student in the class is having some very bad feelings. It is not fair for one person to ridicule another for having strong religious beliefs or for being a member of an ethnic minority. Now, class, how do you think we should treat other persons who are not exactly the same as we are?" Quite a lively discussion ensued. Students cited other examples of intolerance, explained what they thought was wrong with it, and suggested some rules for conduct. Before the end of the class, the students identified and agreed to abide by three rules: "(1) Never make fun of another person in the class. (2) Don't be mean. (3) No stealing." Mrs. Mater subsequently printed the rules on poster board and mounted the sign at the front of the room. She often refers to the rules to remind students about appropriate behavior. After this incident, Mrs. Mater told a colleague, "Maybe my students won't perform the best on the achievement tests. But, by golly, they are going to know how to live with each other and respect each other's feelings."

5.   Seamus Fogarty is inquisitive, and he hopes to instill an inquisitive spirit in his students. To him, the world is a series of puzzles to be solved. He knows that he can rely on textbooks to report how someone else had discovered something, yet the recall of someone else's discovery will not prepare a student to make discoveries of her own. Mr. Fogarty also recognizes that discoveries are seldom haphazard or serendipitous. Discoveries involve purpose, method, observation, industry, and insight. Mr. Fogarty avoids having students memorize reports about the accomplishments of others; instead, he creates situations where students discover problems, attempt solutions, and reflect upon their attempts.

In one representative lesson, Mr. Fogarty began his psychology class by reading aloud an article from the *Washington Post*. The writer reported that a study sponsored by a perfume manufacturer indicated that there was a very strong correlation between the use of scents (colognes, after shave, perfumes) and one's sociability. The researchers defined *sociability* as one's inclination for positive social interactions, such as attending parties, going on dates, and gathering with friends. One's degree of sociability was defined by responses to a survey. The researchers calculated the correlation between the sociability score and the number of instances that a subject wore a scent during a typical week. The newspaper writer concluded the article by recommending that readers should "wear cologne, after shave, or perfume every day if you want to be popular and have many friends." Mr. Fogarty invited his students to comment on the article. For about ten minutes the students asked questions about the methodology of the research and disputed the writer's parting conclusion. Several students cited examples of persons they knew who never wore scents yet were very popular. Mr. Fogarty then asked, "How would we be able to investigate the value and meaning of the study?" Some students suggested that the class conduct a study of its own. "If we are going to conduct a similar study," said Mr. Fogarty, "we need to know something about correlations."

Some proficient math students explained what *correlations* are and described how to calculate them. Mr. Fogarty then used a small data set to model the calculation and determine the significance of the coefficient. He then organized the students into six groups and provided them with other data (for example, rushing yardage and won-lost record). Each group calculated the correlation, with the help of a scientific calculator and with Mr. Fogarty's guidance. In the next lesson, each group reported their findings to the rest of the class and explained whether one factor caused another. Other students from other groups questioned some of the conclusions, and the class worked toward clarifying their concept of correlation. Next, Mr. Fogarty asked each group to design its own experiment: "If the wearing of scents does not cause someone's popularity or influence personality, what does?"

As the lessons progressed, the students posed hypotheses, composed surveys, tested surveys, revised their surveys, collected data, and discussed their findings. Groups reported their study and findings to the rest of the class. In the end, each student wrote a letter to the writer of the *Washington Post* article. In their letters, the students evaluated the value and methodology of the original study, commented on the newswriter's conclusions, and explained their understanding of factors that shape personality and influence popularity.

6.   Lisa Carr considers herself someone who creates an environment for learning. She engages students in thought-provoking activities and considers herself the facilitator for the students' learning experiences. She does not want to be the font of knowledge that transmits information to passive students. Instead, she expects to have students work with each other in completing problem-based activities.

Recently, she had her first period class write in their journals a response to the following prompt: "What are all the images and words that you associate with the word *father?*" The students first worked individually to write a response. Then Ms. Carr called on volunteers to share their ideas. Several students contributed. Next, Ms. Carr distributed an "opinionnaire" which offered a series of statements about an ideal father. For example, one statement said, "A father will provide for and protect his family." In each case, the students indicated whether they agreed or disagreed, responding on a 4-point scale. Ms. Carr then organized the students into groups of three to discuss the judgments they made. Most groups engaged in a lively discussion. Ms. Carr next called on a volunteer to tabulate the students' responses to each item on the opinionnaire. Using a transparency of the opinionnaire and the overhead projector, the student counted the different responses to each item and recorded the totals on the transparency. After this process was completed, Ms. Carr asked the class to write a paragraph about the following questions: "According to our class, what is an ideal father?" The students wrote for much of the balance of the period. At the end of the lesson, Ms. Carr said, "Keeping in mind the class's observations about the ideal father, find pictures from magazines and newspapers that would illustrate those ideas. Have your pictures in class tomorrow."

For the next class meeting, Ms. Carr had boxes of old magazines available in class. She also had poster boards, scissors, and glue sticks. She instructed the students to work in groups of three to create collages to represent the class's ideas about the ideal father. The students selected their own groups and worked diligently for forty minutes. Ms. Carr then called on volunteers to present their collage and explain the images to the class.

For the next period, Ms. Carr distributed copies of several poems about fathers. The poems by such poets as Sylvia Plath, Theodore Roethke, Gwendolyn Brooks, and Allen Ginsberg provided a variety of images of a father. Ms. Carr had the students work in pairs to select a poem and present an oral interpretation. Students selected their own partners, picked a poem, and prepared a reading of it. After working with partners for fifteen minutes, the students presented their interpretation.

For the next three class meetings, Ms. Carr showed the class a DVD of the classic 1947 film, *Life with Father,* starring William Powell, and based on the play by Lindsay and Crouse. Fifteen minutes of class time remained after the third day of viewing. Ms. Carr engaged the class in a large group discussion about whether or not the film provided a realistic or, to their minds, an idealistic view of a father.

Ms. Carr distributed copies of stories about fatherhood by various authors: Mark Twain, Kate Chopin, Mary Wollstonecroft, Garrison Keillor, Guy du Maupaussant, and Kurt Vonnegut. Each group of four students received a different story. In small groups, the students planned an oral presentation about the story. Ms. Carr provided two guidelines: Each group had to convey what happens in the story and characterize the depiction of fatherhood. The students chose a variety of means to tell the story—acting out a skit, offering a puppet show, performing a musical interpretation, giving a simple speech, and providing a graphic representation with the aid of a computer and an LCD panel.

Next, Ms. Carr showed the class clips from three television depictions of fathers: *Father Knows Best, Leave It to Beaver,* and *The Cosby Show.* After the class viewed the video segments, Ms. Carr led the students in a discussion based on the following question: Do these TV shows offer an ideal view of fatherhood?

At the end of Ms. Carr's unit on fatherhood, her students wrote an essay in response to the following prompt. "George Washington is often referred to as the father of our country. Based on what you know about fathers and about Washington, discuss what the phrase means. Is it appropriate to call Washington the father of our country? Does he represent an ideal father? Explain." The essay represented the summative evaluation for the unit.

Resource B

Framework for Observing Classes

(Discussed in Chapters 2 and 3)

Class/Subject: _____

Grade: _____

1. Characterize the *rapport* with students and the general classroom environment.

2. What evidence do you see that the teacher has *planned* for the lesson?

3. Characterize the students' level of *engagement* in the lesson. What evidence do you notice that the students are engaged in the lesson?

4. What *materials* were used as the basis for the learning activities? To what extent do the materials align with goals and seem appropriate for the specific learners?

5. What were the *patterns of discourse* you observed? (e.g., teacher-dominated? student recitation? students engaged with each other in authentic discussion?)

6. If students are actively engaged in the lesson, how *significant* are the apparent goals and activities?

7. What evidence did you see that the teacher *differentiated* for the particular group of students and for individual students within the class?

8. How did the teacher *monitor* students' engagement and their understanding?

Resource C

Student Forum Questions

(Discussed in Chapter 3)

1. Tell me about the class in your schedule where you learn the most?

2. What is special (different, distinctive) about this class?

3. When students need help with their school work, how can they get help in your school?

4. How do you prepare for tests in your classes?

5. What would you have liked to have seen, but didn't get, from your classes at your school?

Resource D

Teacher Interview Questions

(Discussed in Chapters 3 and 7)

Subject: _____

1. Please tell me about the curriculum for the classes that you teach. Think about how you would share descriptions with parents during a "Curriculum Night." What would you offer as a summary description?

2. What are the essential concepts and priority goals that guide the curriculum?

3. How were the priority goals determined (e.g., state standards, committee deliberation, textbooks, state tests)?

4. How is the curriculum organized or sequenced, both within an individual course and across the set of courses within the program?

5. What materials are used, and how were those materials selected?

6. What kind of instructional activities would I typically see if I walked into your class on any given day?

7. To what extent do state standards and state tests drive the activities in your classes?

8. How is articulation and alignment across grades and programs accomplished?

9. What other observations would you like to make about the school's instructional program?

References

Achievement Gap Initiative. (2009). *How high schools become exemplary: Ways that leadership raises achievement and narrows gaps by improving instruction in 15 public high schools.* Cambridge, MA: Harvard University.

Argyris, C., & Schön, D. (1978). *Organisational learning: A theory of action perspective.* Reading, MA: Addison-Wesley.

Azinger, A. T., & Baker, P. J. (2003, July/August). Measures short on follow-through. *Illinois School Board Journal.* Retrieved from http://archives.iasb .com/journal/j3070805.htm

Blank, R. K., & de las Alas, N. (2009). *Effects of teacher professional development on gains in student achievement: How meta-analysis provides evidence useful to education leaders.* Retrieved from http://www.ccsso.org/Documents/2009/ Effects_of_Teacher_Professional_2009.pdf

Borko, H. (2004, November). Professional development and teacher learning: Mapping the terrain. *Educational Researcher, 33*(8), 3–15.

Boyd, D., Lankford, H., Loeb, S., Rockoff, J., & Wyckoff, J. (2008). *The narrowing gap in New York City teacher qualifications and its implications for student achievement in high-poverty schools.* Washington, DC: Urban Institute.

Chinn, C. A., & Malhotra, B. A. (2002, March). Epistemologically authentic inquiry in schools: A theoretical framework for evaluating inquiry tasks. *Science Education, 86*(2), 175–218.

Clotfelter, C. T., Ladd, H. F., & Vigdor, J. L. (2007). *How and why do teacher credentials matter for student achievement?* Durham, NC: Sanford Institute.

Coburn, C. E. (2001). Collective sensemaking about reading: How teachers mediate reading policy in their professional communities. *Educational Evaluation and Policy Analysis, 23*(2), 145–170.

Coburn, C. E. (2005, July). Shaping teacher sensemaking: School leaders and the enactment of reading policy. *Educational Policy, 19*(3), 476–509.

Coburn, C. E., & Russell, J. L. (2008, September). District policy and teachers' social networks. *Educational Evaluation and Policy Analysis, 30*(3), 203–235.

Cohen, D. K. (1990, December). A revolution in one classroom: The case of Mrs. Oublier. *Educational Evaluation and Policy Analysis, 12*(3), 327–345.

Cohen, D. K., & Hill, H. C. (2000, January). Instructional policy and classroom performance: The mathematics reform in California. *Teachers College Record, 102*, 294–343.

Cohen, D. K., Raudenbush, S. W., & Ball, D. L. (2003, July). Resources, instruction, and research. *Educational Evaluation and Policy Analysis, 25*(2), 119–142.

Cohen, D. K., & Spillane, J. P. (1992, January). Policy and practice: The relations between governance and instruction. *Review of Research in Education, 18,* 3–49.

Csikszentmihalyi, Mihaly. (1990). *Flow: The psychology of optimal experience.* New York, NY: HarperCollins.

Csikszentmihalyi, M., & Schneider, B. L. (2000). *Becoming adult: How teenagers prepare for the world of work.* New York: Basic Books.

Daniels, H., & Bizar, M. (2004). *Teaching the best practice way: Methods that matter, K–12.* Portland, ME: Stenhouse Press.

Daniels, H., Zemelman, S., & Hyde, A. (2005). *Best practice: Today's standards for teaching and learning in America's schools* (3rd ed.). Portsmouth, NH: Heinemann.

Danielson, C. (1996). *Enhancing professional practice: A framework for teaching.* Alexandria, VA: ASCD.

Danielson, C. (2007). *Enhancing professional practice: A framework for teaching* (2nd ed.). Alexandria, VA: ASCD.

Danielson, C., & McGreal, T. L. (2000). *Teacher evaluation to enhance professional practice.* Alexandria, VA: ASCD.

Darling-Hammond, L. (2000). Teacher quality and student achievement: A review of state policy evidence. *Educational Policy Analysis Archives, 8*(1). Retrieved from: http://epaa.asu.edu/epaa/v8n1

Darling-Hammond, L., & Bransford, J. (2005). *Preparing teachers for a changing world: What teachers should learn and be able to do.* San Francisco, CA: Jossey-Bass.

Darling-Hammond, L., & Haselkorn, D. (2009, April). Reforming teaching: Are we missing the boat? *Education Week, 28*(27), 36.

Deci, E. (1971). Effects of externally mediated rewards on intrinsic motivation. *Journal of Personality and Social Psychology, 18,* 105–115.

Deci, E., Koestner, R., & Ryan, R. M. (2001, March). Extrinsic rewards and intrinsic motivation in education: Reconsidered once again. *Review of Educational Research, 71*(1), 1–27.

Desimone, L. M., Porter, A. C., Garet, M. S., Yoon, K. S., & Birman, B. F. (2002, January). Effects of professional development on teachers' instruction: Results from a three-year longitudinal study. *Educational Evaluation and Policy Analysis, 24*(2), 81–112.

Dewey, J. (1938). *Logic: The theory of inquiry.* New York, NY: Henry Holt.

Fenstermacher, G. D., & Richardson, V. (2005). On making determinations of quality in teaching. *Teachers College Record, 107*(1), 186–213.

Gallwey, W. T. (1986). *The inner game of tennis.* New York, NY: Bantam.

Gallwey, W. T. (2001). *The inner game of work: Focus, learning, pleasure, and mobility in the workplace.* New York, NY: Random House.

Garet, M. S., Porter, A. C., Desimone, L., Birman, B. F., & Yoon, K. S. (2001, January). What makes professional development effective? Results from a national sample of teachers. *American Educational Research Journal, 38*(4), 915–945.

Gee, J. P. (2007). *What video games have to teach us about learning and literacy* (2nd ed.). New York, NY: Palgrave Macmillan.

Goodlad, J. I. (1984). *A place called school: Prospects for the future. (A study of schooling in the United States).* New York, NY: McGraw-Hill.

Graham, S., & Perin, D. (2007). *Writing next: Effective strategies to improve writing of adolescents in middle and high schools—A report to Carnegie Corporation of New York.* Washington, DC: Alliance for Excellent Education.

Graham, S., & Perin, D. (2007). A meta-analysis of writing instruction for adolescent students. *Journal of Educational Psychology, 99,* 445–476.

Grossman, P. L., & Stodolsky, S. S. (1995). Content as context: The role of school subjects in secondary school teaching. *Educational Researcher, 24*(8), 5–23.

Hargreaves, A. (1991). *Contrived collegiality: The micropolitics of teacher collaboration.* In J. Blasé (Ed.), *The politics of life in schools: Power, conflict, and cooperation* (pp. 46–72). Newbury Park, CA: Sage.

Hargreaves, A., & Fullan, M. (1992). *Understanding teacher development.* New York, NY: Teachers College Press.

Harlow, H. F. (1950). Learning and satiation of response in intrinsically motivated complex puzzled performance by monkeys. *Journal of Comparative and Physiological Psychology, 43,* 289–294.

Hill, H. C., Blunk, M. L., Charalambos, C. Y., Lewis, J. M., Phelps, G. C., Sleep, L., & Ball, D. L. (2008). Mathematical knowledge for teaching and mathematical quality of instruction: An exploratory study. *Cognition and Instruction, 26*(4), 430–511.

Hillocks, G., Jr. (2009a, July). Some practices and approaches are clearly better than others and we had better not ignore the differences. *English Journal, 98*(6), 23–29.

Hillocks, G., Jr. (2009b, August). Needed: A revolution in the teaching of literacy. *English Leadership Quarterly, 32*(1), 8–12.

Ingersoll, R. M., & Smith, T. M. (2003, May). The wrong solution to the teacher shortage. *Educational Leadership, 60*(8), 30–33.

Jackson, P. (1996). *Sacred hoops.* New York, NY: Hyperion.

Jackson, P. W. (1968). *Life in classrooms.* New York, NY: Teachers College Press.

Jackson, P. W. (1986). *The practice of teaching.* New York, NY: Teachers College Press.

Jones, A. C. (1985). *Content analysis of teacher dismissal cases for incompetence under the Illinois Tenure Teacher Hearing Officer Act, 1975–1983.* Chicago, IL: Loyola University.

Joyner, E. T. (2000). *No more "drive-by" staff development.* In P. Senge, N. Cambron-McCabe, T. Lucas, B. Smith, J. Dutton, & A. Kleiner (Eds.), *Schools that learn: A fifth discipline fieldbook for educators, parents, and everyone who cares about education* (pp. 385–394). New York, NY: Doubleday.

Kachur, D., Stout, D., & Edwards, C. (2010). *Classroom walkthroughs to improve teaching and learning.* Larchmont, NY: Eyes on Education.

Kelling, G., & Coles, C. (1996). *Fixing broken windows: Restoring order and reducing crime in our communities.* New York, NY: Free Press.

Kennedy, M. M. (2005). *Inside teaching: How classroom life undermines reform.* Cambridge, MA: Harvard University Press.

Kliebard, H. M. (1987). *The struggle for the American curriculum, 1893–1958.* New York, NY: Routledge & Kegan Paul.

Knowles, M. S., Swanson, R. A., & Holton, E. F. (2005). *The adult learner: The definitive classic in adult education and human resource development* (6th ed.). Burlington, MA: Butterworth-Heinemann.

Labaree, D. F. (2000). Resisting educational standards. *Phi Delta Kappan, 82*(1), 28–33.

Langer, J. A. (2001, January). Beating the odds: Teaching middle and high school students to read and write well. *American Educational Research Journal, 38*(4), 837–880.

Levine, S. L. (1988). *Promoting adult growth in schools: The promise of professional development.* Boston, MA: Allyn & Bacon.

Linn, M. C., & Muilenburg, L. (1996, January). Creating lifelong science learners: What models form a firm foundation? *Educational Researcher, 25*(5), 18–24.

Lipton, L., & Wellman, B. (2002). *Mentoring matters: A practical guide to learning-focused relationships.* Sherman, CT: Mira Via.

Little, J. W. (1989, January). District policy choices and teacher's professional development opportunities. *Educational Evaluation and Policy Analysis, 11*(2), 165–179.

Little, J. W. (1993, January). Teachers' professional development in a climate of educational reform. *Educational Evaluation and Policy Analysis, 15*(2), 129–151.

Lortie, D. C. (1975). *Schoolteacher: A sociological study.* Chicago, IL: University of Chicago Press.

Marzano, R. J. (2003). *What works in schools: Translating research into action.* Alexandria, VA: ASCD.

Marzano, R. J. (2004). *Building background knowledge for academic achievement: Research on what works in schools.* Alexandria, VA: ASCD.

McCann, T. M., Ressler, P., Chambers, D., & Minor, J. (2010, October). Teaching English together: Leadership through collaboration. *English Leadership Quarterly, 33*(2), 10–13.

McCann, T. M., Jones, A. C., & Aronoff, G. (2010). Truths hidden in plain view. *Phi Delta Kappan. 92*(2), 65–67.

McCann, T. M., Johannessen, L. R., & Ricca, B. (2005). *Supporting beginning English teachers: Research and implications for teacher induction.* Urbana, IL: National Council of Teachers of English.

Merriam, S. B., & Caffarella, R. S. (1999). *Learning in adulthood: A comprehensive guide.* San Francisco, CA: Jossey-Bass.

Newmann, F. M., Smith, B., Allensworth, E., & Bryk, A. S. (2001). Instructional program coherence: What it is and why it should guide school improvement policy. *Educational Evaluation and Policy Analysis, 23*(4), 297–321.

Nystrand, M. (2006). Research on the role of classroom discourse as it affects reading comprehension. *Research in the Teaching of English, 40*(4), 392–412.

Nystrand, M., with A. Gamoran, R. Kachur, & C. Prendergast. (1997). *Opening dialogue: Understanding the dynamics of language and learning in the English classroom.* New York, NY: Teachers College Press.

Pink, D. H. (2009). *Drive: The surprising truth about what motivates us.* New York, NY: Riverhead Books.

Pintrich, P. R., Marx, R. W., & Boyle, R. A. (1993, January). Beyond cold conceptual change: The role of motivational beliefs and classroom contextual factors in the process of conceptual change. *Review of Educational Research, 63*(2), 167-199.

Pitton, D. E. (2006). *Mentoring novice teachers: Fostering a dialogue process* (2nd ed.). Thousand Oaks, CA: Corwin.

Richardson, J. (2001). Seeing through new eyes: Walk throughs offer news ways to view schools. *Tools for Schools.* Retrieved from http://www.nsdc.org/library/publications/tools/tools10–01rich.cfm

Riordan, J. E., & Noyce, P. E. (2001, July). The impact of two standards-based mathematics curricula on student achievement in Massachusetts. *Journal for Research in Mathematics Education, 32*(4), 368–398.

Rowan, B. (2000). *Teachers work and instructional management, Part 1: Alternative view of the task of teaching.* In W. Hoy and C. G. Miskel (Eds.), *Theory and research in educational administration* (Vol. 1, pp. 129–149), Greenwich, CT: Information Age.

Rowley, J. B. (1999, May). The good mentor. *Educational Leadership. 56*(8), 20–22.

Sarason, S. B. (2004). *And what do you mean by learning?* Portsmouth, NH: Heinemann.

Saxe, G. B., Gearhart, M., & Nasir, N. S. (2001, January). Enhancing students' understanding of mathematics: A study of three contrasting approaches to professional support. *Journal of Mathematics Teacher Education, 4*(1), 55–79.

Secada, W. G., Wehlage, G., & Newmann, F. M. (1995). *A guide to authentic instruction and assessment: Vision, standards and scoring.* Madison: Wisconsin Center for Education Research.

Severson, K. (2011, July 5). Systematic cheating is found in Atlanta's school system. *New York Times.* Retrieved from: http://www.nytimes.com/2011/07/06/education/06atlanta.html?_r=1&scp=2&sq=Atlanta%20public%20schools&st=cse

Smagorinsky, P. (2009, July). Is it time to abandon the idea of "best practices" in the teaching of English? *English Journal, 98*(6), 15–22.

Smith, B. A., Allensworth, E., Bryk, A. S., & Newmann, F. M. (2001). Instructional program coherence: What it is and why it should guide school improvement policy. *Educational Evaluation and Policy Analysis, 23*(4), 297–321.

Spillane, J. P., & Jennings, N. E. (1997). Aligned instructional policy and ambitious pedagogy: Exploring instructional reform from the classroom perspective. *Teachers College Record, 98*(3), 449–481.

Stein, M. K., & Coburn, C. E. (2008, August). Architectures for learning: A comparative analysis of two urban school districts. *American Journal of Education, 114*(4), 583–626.

Stein, M. K., & Nelson, B. S. (2003, January). Leadership content knowledge. *Educational Evaluation and Policy Analysis, 25*(4), 423–448.

Stephens, D., Boldt, G., Clark, C., Gaffney, J., Shelton, J., Story, J., & Weinzierl, J. (2000). Learning about learning from four teachers. *Research in the Teaching of English, 24*(4), 532–565.

Stigler, J. W., & Hiebert, J. (1999). *The teaching gap: Best ideas from the world's teachers for improving education in the classroom.* New York, NY: Free Press.

Stodolsky, S. S., & Grossman, P. L. (1995). The impact of subject matter on curricular activity: An analysis of five academic subjects. *American Educational Research Journal, 32*(2), 227–249.

Stronge, J. (2007). *Qualities of effective teachers.* Alexandria, VA: ASCD.

Toch, T., & Rothman, R. (2008). *Rush to judgment: Teacher evaluation in public education.* Washington, DC: Education Sector.

Tye, B. B. (2000). *Hard truths: Uncovering the deep structure of schooling.* New York: Teachers College Press.

Tye, M. (2000). *Consciousness, color, and content.* Cambridge: MIT Press.

U.S. Department of Labor. (1992). *Learning a living: A blueprint for high performance: A SCANS report for America 2000 : Executive summary.* Washington, DC: Department of Labor.

Valentine, J. (2005). *The instructional practices inventory: A process for profiling student engaged learning for school improvement.* Columbia: University of Missouri. Retrieved from: https://mospace.umsystem.edu/xmlui/bitstream/handle/10355/3564/ProcessProfilingStudentLearning.pdf?sequence=1

Villani, S. (2009). *Comprehensive mentoring programs for new teachers: Models of induction and support* (2nd ed.). Thousand Oaks, CA: Corwin.

Vygotsky, L. (1986). *Thought and language.* Cambridge: MIT Press.

Wei, R. C., Darling-Hammond, L., Andree, A., Richardson, N., & Orphanos, S. (2009). *Professional learning in the learning profession: A status report on teacher development in the United States and abroad.* Dallas, TX: National Staff Development Council.

Wiggins, G., & McTighe, J. (2005). *Understanding by design* (2nd ed.). Alexandria, VA: ASCD.

Willingham, D. T. (2009). *Why don't students like school: A cognitive scientist answers questions about how the mind works and what it means for the classroom.* San Francisco, CA: Jossey-Bass.

Wilson, J. Q. (1989). *Bureaucracy: What government agencies do and why they do it.* New York, NY: Basic Books.

Wilson, S., Floden, R., & Ferrini-Mundy, J. (2001). *Teacher preparation research: Current knowledge, gaps, and recommendations.* Seattle: University of Washington.

Windschitl, M. (2002). Framing constructivism in practice as the negotiation of dilemmas: An analysis of the conceptual, pedagogical, cultural, and political challenges facing teachers. *Review of Educational Research, 72*(2), 131–175.

Index

CORWIN
A SAGE Company

The Corwin logo—a raven striding across an open book—represents the union of courage and learning. Corwin is committed to improving education for all learners by publishing books and other professional development resources for those serving the field of PreK–12 education. By providing practical, hands-on materials, Corwin continues to carry out the promise of its motto: **"Helping Educators Do Their Work Better."**

Advancing professional learning for student success

Learning Forward (formerly National Staff Development Council) is an international association of learning educators committed to one purpose in K–12 education: Every educator engages in effective professional learning every day so every student achieves.